15 1

1 28

SOCIAL SECURITY AND THE BUDGET

Proceedings of the First Conference of the National Academy of Social Insurance

Washington, D.C.

Edited by
Henry J. Aaron

UNIVERSITY
PRESS OF
AMERICA

Lanham • New York • London

NATIONAL
ACADEMY
OF • SOCIAL
INSURANCE

Copyright © 1990 by

The National Academy of Social Insurance

University Press of America®, Inc.

4720 Boston Way
Lanham, MD 20706

3 Henrietta Street
London WC2E 8LU England

Printed in the United States of America

British Cataloging in Publication Information Available

Co-published by arrangement with the
National Academy of Social Insurance

Library of Congress Cataloging-in-Publication Data

National Academy of Social Insurance (U.S.).
Conference (1st : 1988 : Washington, D.C.)
Social Security and the budget : proceedings of the
First Conference of the National Academy of Social Insurance,
December 15 and 16, 1988, Washington, D.C. / Henry J. Aaron, editor.
p.   cm.
1. Social security—United States—Finance—Congresses.   2. Budget
deficits—United States—Congresses.   I. Aaron, Henry J.   II. Title.
HD7125.N28   1988   353.0083'56—dc20   89–22570 CIP

ISBN 0–8191–7601–X (alk. paper)
ISBN 0–8191–7602–8 (pbk. : alk. paper)

The paper used in this publication meets the minimum requirements of American
National Standard for Information Sciences—Permanence of Paper for Printed
Library Materials, ANSI Z39.48–1984.

THE NATIONAL ACADEMY OF
SOCIAL INSURANCE

THE NATIONAL ACADEMY OF SOCIAL INSURANCE IS A nonprofit, nonpartisan organization devoted to furthering knowledge and understanding of Social Security and related public and private programs. The Academy was incorporated in 1986 and received start-up funding from the Carnegie Corporation of New York, the Edna McConnell Clark Foundation, the Marshall Field Foundation's Study Group on Social Security, the Villers Foundation and several individuals. In 1987, the Academy hired an Executive Director and established an office in Washington, D.C. In 1988, it invited 122 Founding Members and launched its program activities, one of which was this Conference.

The Academy takes responsibility for assuring the independence of any project organized under its auspices. Participants in the conference were chosen for their recognized expertise and with due consideration of the balance of disciplines appropriate to the program. The resulting proceedings represent the views of the those who presented them and are not the views of the members or officers of the National Academy of Social Insurance.

ACKNOWLEDGMENTS

MANY PEOPLE WERE INSTRUMENTAL IN TURNING THE First Annual Meeting of the National Academy of Social Insurance into this book. The planning committee for the conference, which I chaired, included Robert M. Ball, Alicia H. Munnell and Lawrence H. Thompson. Pamela J. Larson, Executive Director of the National Academy of Social Insurance, and her staff, Sara M. Berman and Willieree T. Murray, prepared the manuscript for publication. Copyediting was contributed by Joan Poskanzer of the Federal Reserve Bank of Boston. The Conference was supported, in part, by a grant from the Alfred P. Sloan Foundation.   H.A.

ACKNOWLEDGMENTS

CONTENTS

SOCIAL SECURITY AND THE BUDGET: AN OVERVIEW

Henry J. Aaron*

S OCIAL SECURITY AND THE BUDGET ARE MUCH ON THE minds of members of Congress and the public. Growth of the Federal debt has been unprecedented. At the same time, the Social Security reserves are larger than ever and increasing fast.

In the early 1980s, Social Security experienced a short-term financing crisis. The National Commission on Social Security Reform, organized by President Reagan and chaired by Alan Greenspan, proposed a series of changes most of which Congress enacted. The short-term crisis was resolved and trust fund reserves began to grow. These reserves were seen as a cushion to help meet the costs of benefits for the baby boom generation, whose retirement will begin early in the twenty-first century.

The Greenspan commission did not project economic growth to be as rapid as it turned out to be and therefore underestimated the accumulation of reserves. Paradoxically, however, the commission was more optimistic about the long-run balance between revenues and expenditures than current projections. At the same time that both reserve accumulation and the projected need for those reserves have surpassed expectations, federal deficits on other operations of government have reached unprecedented levels. Because Social Security reserves are included in the Gramm-Rudman-Hollings deficit reduction targets, a surplus in the Social Security trust fund makes a deficit in the general revenues look smaller than it actually is. By the end of 1988, Social Security reserves totaled $104 billion.

On December 15 and 16, 1988, the National Academy of Social Insurance held a two-day conference on the relationship between Social Security and the deficit, as part of its First Annual Meeting. More than 200 social

---

*Senior Fellow, The Brookings Institution.

insurance experts, policy analysts, members of Congress and their staff, executive branch staff and business and labor leaders came to the Washington Court Hotel in Washington, D.C. to participate in the event.

The program examined four topic areas: "Setting Long-Run Deficit Reduction Targets: The Politics of Budget Design," "Costs of the Aging Population: Implications for Current Budget Policy," "Public Opinion on Social Security and the Budget," and "Formulating a Deficit Reduction Package: What Is the Role of Social Security?" This overview briefly summarizes the conference papers and discussion.

Setting Long-Run Deficit Reduction Targets: The Politics of Budget Design

Charles Schultze argued that budget policy should be fashioned to promote an increase in the national saving rate. Such an increase is needed now, according to Schultze, in order to accumulate productive wealth and raise incomes to a level that will enable the current working generation to meet its retirement and health care needs without imposing undue burdens on the next generation.

Schultze warned, however, that national saving will not rise if the Social Security reserves are used on outlays for current programs. The national saving rate needed to sustain the current rate of productivity growth through the next decade would require private saving to be maintained at today's rate if the budget deficit is reduced to about 1 percent of national income. Additional saving is required if the current generation of workers is to pay for its own Social Security benefits.

Schultze argues that the current budget deficit ought to be cut in two stages: Over the next four years, the total federal budget, including additions to Social Security reserves, should be brought into balance. Over the subsequent four to five years the federal budget, excluding additions to Social Security reserves, should be balanced.

Lawrence Thompson concurred with Schultze's economic analysis but pointed out that Social Security reserves could be viewed in at least two ways, from the standpoint of either the Social Security program or the economy at large. Increased national saving means greater total output, which would make the costs of retirement benefits for this large baby boom cohort less burdensome. But, Thompson pointed out, the drop in the ratio of workers to retirees is not a temporary event. Nor are generations in the mid twenty-first century likely to appreciate the fact that they are better off because of added saving in the late twentieth century. So increasing national saving will have little political effect when costs actually rise.

According to Thompson, Schultze's arguments rest on several tacit assumptions: that national saving should be increased for reasons that have nothing to do with Social Security, that large reserves will not motivate undesirable program changes, and that an increase in national saving now will not be eroded by a drop in saving in the future. Under these conditions, Thompson agreed with Schultze's prescription.

Rudolph Penner also agreed that an increased national saving rate would be desirable and that increased public saving would not lower private saving. He questioned whether moving additions to OASDI reserves off-budget would motivate more total deficit reduction.

Penner expressed fear that taking Social Security totally off-budget would lead to benefit increases that would not count against the "official budget deficit" and would dissipate the reserve. Furthermore, incentives to find savings, especially in Medicare, would be diminished if those savings do not count toward deficit reduction.

Congress, according to Penner, needs to know how much it is relying on private capital markets and a unified budget deficit is perhaps the most exact measure. In short, Penner agreed with Schultze's economics but disagreed with his politics.

Costs of the Aging Population: Implications for Current Budget Policy

Henry Aaron argued that the commonly cited increase in the ratio of workers to retirees tells nothing about the economic burdens the elderly will impose. The burdens depend on whether each generation of retirees produces as much as it consumes in its lifetime. The baby boom generation, according to Aaron, will receive in Social Security benefits only what is paid in payroll taxes under current financing plans plus a fair rate of return. However, this generation is not paying enough to cover the future costs of their health and long-term care or the costs of current government consumption. Recent budget policy and inadequate financing of health benefits are imposing burdens on the future.

Aaron suggests that the reserve in the OASDI trust funds holds the potential through increased capital formation of adding to national output more than the additional pension cost that will be generated by the increased number of beneficiaries. He further advocates that Social Security benefits be taxed as private pensions are, that steps be taken to increase saving for health care, and that Federal budget targets be set independently of the Social Security and Medicare trust funds.

Phillip Longman argued that increasing the national saving rate through increased payroll taxes will not lead to greater capital formation and greater productivity. Longman asserted that the rise in regressive payroll taxes to pay future health and retirement benefits will heighten resistance to progressive income taxes, thereby making the necessary reduction of the overall budget deficits more difficult to achieve.

Longman recommended that government mandate individuals to save more toward their own retirement than under current policy. Wealthy citizens would be compelled to save a greater share of their income than the poor. Longman also recommended dramatic increases in the age at which Social Security and Medicare benefits can be claimed. Such changes, he asserted, would boost private investment, increase productivity and add to incomes for the younger generation. Longman also claimed that this process would create more generational equity.

Robert Kuttner looked at the politics of the Aaron and Longman papers. He found several reasons to agree with Aaron that additions to the reserves in the Social Security trust fund should not be used to offset deficits elsewhere in the budget. If Social Security is off-budget and the rest of the budget is in balance, the resulting overall surplus raises the nation's saving rate. It also promotes an ideology that the rich do not have to get richer in order to increase saving. Finally, taking Social Security out of the budget would refute the generational equity argument by firmly involving the baby boom generation in Social Security.

Kuttner, however, also agreed with Longman that the payroll tax is not the best way to increase saving, though Kuttner's viewpoint is that Federal Insurance Contributions Act taxes should be supplemented with income from the general revenues. Any increase in savings, voluntary (via Longman) or mandatory (via Aaron), will decrease current consumption. Social Security is simply more effective and efficient at providing benefits.

Kuttner held that Longman's generational equity argument is really an ideological critique of Social Security. Longman, and others with his view, are not debating old versus young but rather laissez-faire versus mixed economy. Kuttner pointed out that proponents of the generational equity argument do not suggest taking social insurance away from the old to give it to the young. Rather they suggest taking it away from the old to free up tax dollars for investment in the private sector, in hopes that it will trickle down to the nation's children.

John Shoven examined the economics of the papers presented. Because of the low national saving rate, the high trade deficit and the national debt, Shoven favored Aaron's push for an increase in the nation's saving rate. However, he maintained that Aaron downplayed the importance of the "horrible ratios" of workers to retirees. Depending on how you fund retirement benefits, the ratios affect different cohorts in different ways, but they do have a very real effect.

Currently the baby boom generation is helping to finance today's retirees as well as its own retirement. To ease the retirement strain, Shoven would recommend that some of the pressure be taken off the baby boom generation and put on today's retirees by accelerating the rise in the retirement age. At the same time, however, the baby boom generation has been on a "consumption and borrowing binge." Overall, the baby boom generation does not appear to be making great sacrifices.

In conclusion, Shoven advocated an increase in national saving, an increase in private saving, and elimination of the Federal debt. The problem today, stressed Shoven, is overall fiscal policy, not Social Security.

Public Opinion on Social Security and the Budget

According to research presented by Fay Lomax Cook, the public and members of the U.S. House of Representatives overwhelmingly support policies that maintain or increase Social Security benefits. The general public wants increased benefits, while Congressional representatives prefer maintaining benefits at their current level (adjusting for cost-of-living increases).

The public's support for Social Security rests on two beliefs: that all of society benefits from Social Security and that the elderly have few alternative sources of income. Cook points out that support from the public could change if these perceptions were altered.

Members of the U.S. House of Representatives who were interviewed all indicated support for the program. This support, however, masks two belief structures. Some support the program because they have highly favorable attitudes toward Social Security. Others have strong reservations about the program but support it because of their constituents. Cook concludes that on the surface the program looks very safe but the belief structure motivating the public and the division within the House could mean changes in the level of future support.

Karlyn Keene expressed three reservations about Fay Cook's research. Cook compared support for Social Security with support for six other social programs. Keene pointed out that the amount of information respondents had about each program could be very influential in determining the support they will give a program. The research does not reveal the respondents' prior level of information about the programs.

Cook also asked if respondents would be willing to pay higher taxes to maintain or increase benefits and found that most would. Keene pointed out that questions about paying taxes looked at in isolation do not tell policymakers very much. Finally, Keene stated that the general public is perhaps more inclined than are policymakers to increase benefits because the public does not understand the intricacies of policy as well as do members of Congress. Keene concluded that public opinion about Social

Security is based not on an understanding of the program but on an unshakable belief in the value of the program.

Norman Ornstein agreed that support for Social Security is strong. He also has completed research showing the public willing to increase spending on only three of twelve policy areas. One is providing a decent standard of living for the elderly. Ornstein suggested this support for Social Security is motivated by three thoughts: that Social Security gives young adults freedom from having to care for their parents; that there is value in getting something back for what you pay in; and that the program is fair. He expressed concern that the perception of fairness may change as people realize that the payroll tax is the largest tax burden they bear.

Ornstein concluded by pointing out that in the current budget debate we must ask if we are going to increase general revenues or cut programs. Will cost-of-living increases be cut? What should we do with the growing surplus? Ornstein suggested that increased taxation of benefits and reduced regressivity of payroll taxes would be desirable changes in the future.

Hugh Heclo characterized Cook's research as a good "still life" of public opinion but he pointed to three trends that could be signs of trouble. The first is the "disappearing windfall." The nature of pension systems is such that those who get in on the early stages of the program get an extremely good deal. Social Security is now 54 years old and, although still a good deal, not as much of one as it once was.

The second trend is the increasing payroll taxes that might be needed to fund Medicare. As this tax burden grows, public support may shrink. Finally, Heclo pointed out that the elderly are no longer seen as needy. As Fay Cook's research suggests, this change in perception could lower support for the program.

Heclo concluded that trouble may lie ahead. He pointed out that no public opinion exists about the growing reserves in the Social Security trust funds. If the public understood that they are currently funding both their own retirement and that of today's elderly, they might not be supportive. Heclo recommended using the reserve to fund programs for children as an investment in the future.

Formulating a Deficit Reduction Package: What Is the Role of Social Security?

This session brought together four experts with diverse backgrounds in Social Security and budget policy. Robert Ball began the discussion by advocating that Social Security not be a part of decisions about short-term deficit reduction decisions at all, because Social Security is a long-term program. Playing with it is bad for the solvency of the program and bad for public confidence in the program. This does not mean that the elderly should not contribute to deficit reduction. It is simply to say that Social Security need not be the vehicle. An increase in the income tax, for all citizens, seems a more appropriate method to Ball.

One change, however, is needed for Social Security and coincidentally would contribute to deficit reduction. That change would be to make Social Security and Medicare universal. And if Social Security had to be a part of a deficit reduction compromise, the best method would be to tax a greater portion of Social Security benefits.

Ball went on to point out that building a huge Social Security reserve does not make sense if it is simply depleted in the middle of the next century. Since the reduction in the ratio of workers to retirees is permanent, it might make sense to build a permanent partial reserve. But Social Security would work equally well as a pay-as-you-go system.

James Jones began by stating that everyone, and everything, will need to be a part of deficit reduction. The Federal debt should be taken seriously because it burdens the next generation and puts our fate in foreign hands. The Social Security reserves, however, should not be raided to lower the deficit. This would only exacerbate the problem. Social Security should be removed immediately from deficit reduction targets.

Jones held that retirees should be, and are, willing to be part of the deficit reduction solution — for example, by reducing payments to suppliers, increasing the tax on pension benefits, and including the subsidy value of Medicare in the tax base. He called for consideration of the option of investing the reserves in the private sector, and of measures to encourage the elderly to remain economically active.

Carol Cox asserted that any deficit reduction plan cannot possibly be taken seriously unless it includes Social Security. Over the past twenty years many social programs have been cut but Social Security has continued to grow. By its sheer size, it is impossible to consider budget policy without considering Social Security. Cox participated in a nationwide series of discussion groups called "Exercise in Hard Choices" and found the public willing to consider cuts in Social Security and Medicare. People do prefer taxing benefits to cutting the cost-of-living adjustment (COLA) but most would do something with the COLA as well. A majority of the American public believes that more money should be targeted on the needy.

Cox held that Social Security cannot be isolated from deficit reduction simply because of its financing mechanism. Programs that have been on the books for fifty years are not scrutinized the way new programs are, but perhaps they should be. When it comes to the bottom line in deficit reduction, we only need marginal changes but, she said, the American public wants to cut spending, including spending on social insurance programs, not raise taxes.

Alan Blinder pointed out that the deficit, although a very big number, is really not the huge problem many make it out to be. The size of the Social Security annual surplus is also not extraordinary when one considers that by 1993 almost one-third of it will be interest earnings. If, in the short term, Social Security is to contribute to deficit reduction, Blinder feels it should be through taxation of benefits.

Over the long run, by the year 2030 the Social Security reserve will be made up almost entirely of interest earnings. The GNP will also be an astronomical number. At that time, a deficit of one and one-quarter percent of GNP (about the historic norm) and a Social Security surplus of about that same amount would be a positive economic scenario.

Blinder concluded that this long-run situation will be easier to create if Social Security is taken off budget in 1993. The only good reason to spend the reserve now would be to invest in new marginal public infrastructure or human capital. However, Blinder was doubtful that any such investment really would be more than a paper transaction, and therefore he saw more good coming from removing Social Security from the budget.

Conclusion

The conclusion from the panel discussions, as well as from the rest of the conference, is that even though individuals hold widely different philosophical views about Social Security, they are often able to agree on specific policies relating to the program. This agreement was evident in the substantial support among the conference participants for further taxing Social Security benefits and for using any build up in the Social Security trust fund to increase national saving.

It is the hope of the National Academy of Social Insurance that this Conference advanced the Social Security debate through challenging presentations and open discussion among America's social insurance experts. These proceedings can now extend that discussion to a broader audience.

INTRODUCTORY REMARKS

The Honorable John Heinz*

I T IS A GREAT HONOR TO DELIVER THE FIRST SPEECH TO the first annual meeting of such a distinguished group of Social Security experts. Having just come off the campaign trail, I know firsthand that Social Security policy does not belong solely to the experts. The most vocal—and real—debate over Social Security does not rage in the universities or in the Social Security Administration's offices or even in the Congress. The critical debate over Social Security is carried out in newspapers, on television, and—most of all—in living rooms and kitchens across America. No matter how secure or immune from politics we want Social Security to be, any program that withholds thousands of dollars a year from every worker's wages to pay every sixth American a benefit will always be in critical condition. The tension in this program between taxpayers and beneficiaries is not unique to the "me-too" generation or the demographic bulge of the baby boom generation. It is built into the program by design. It is a tension balanced by the Congress, and this balancing act will be with us into the indefinite future.

The mission of the Academy is to investigate, evaluate and inform. This is a formidable challenge especially because it is important to educate, not just the members of Congress, but the people who elect us as well. Even with the best of intentions about Social Security *policy*, it is easy for us to lose our bearings in the stormy seas of Social Security *politics*. Buffeted by the threat of negative campaigns, the fear of single-issue senior voters (which these days means anyone 50 or older), or the danger of a revolt of the baby boom generation (which is everyone around 40 or younger), it is often difficult to know where a safe harbor of Social Security policy really lies. The light that the National Academy can shed through debate, study,

---

*United States Senator from Pennsylvania.

research, and public education will be critical to this process. I congratulate Bob Ball and the other founding fathers and mothers for having brought the Academy into this world. I am honored to be a part of it. And I am pleased that you have chosen to charge it with an active role in framing the public debate.

Your superb insight and good judgment is especially evident in the choice of a topic for your first annual meeting. The role of Social Security in the Federal budget has been a favorite topic of mine ever since I worked with many of you on the National Commission in 1982. And it is one place where the public is considerably ahead of the Congress in its concern about the issue. Six years ago, when Social Security was running deficits of $8 billion a year, the public wanted Social Security out of the Federal budget to protect it from congressional budget cuts. Today, in the context of a fiscal year 1989 Social Security operating surplus of $45 billion, my constituents tell me overwhelmingly that they don't want these annual additions to the reserves for future retirees lent and then spent, now, to mask a hidden budget deficit and make today's politicians look good. In response to a recent "sample ballot" I sent out in Pennsylvania, 99.91 percent of the 80,000 constituents who responded—a group including younger people as well as seniors—told me they wanted Social Security taken out of the Gramm-Rudman-Hollings calculations of deficit reduction targets, even though they understood the effect it would have on the deficit.

This public sentiment has been clear all along, but it has been difficult to convince policymakers that there was any reason to worry eight or ten years ago about the effects and implications of Social Security's deficits, and now about the even larger and growing surpluses. Until recently, many of my colleagues have viewed it as simply an accounting question—one of little consequence. Even now, as seemingly every editor and Op-Ed writer in the country is working on an article about the serious policy implications of how we handle Social Security's mounting reserves, a considerable number of my colleagues worry that it would be too hard to remove Social Security numbers—which specifically include counting all revenues to Social Security as general revenues—from the budget and the way we report the deficit. Instead, they are willing to rationalize this deficit deception by saying we can do the right thing later—but not *now!*

Is this only a case of a small fiscal fix? Why do we care whether Social Security revenues are included in the Gramm-Rudman-Hollings deficit reduction targets? What difference does it really make? To the extent that Congress continues to make expenditures for general government purposes that further exceed general revenues, it makes a big difference, the import of which is significant, the consequences most severe and getting *worse.*

This year is a case in point. Congress will try to enact $32 billion of savings or taxes to achieve a Gramm-Rudman-Hollings deficit target of $100 billion for fiscal year 1990. Under current rules and practices, this $100 billion deficit target will only be achieved because of scoring all Social Security revenues and outlays as if they are part of the general fund. Since established Social Security revenues will exceed outlay in fiscal year 1990 by some $63 billion, Congress will be able to avoid that much more in the way of difficult decisions. Instead, Social Security reserves will be lent to—and spent by—the general fund. By 1993, under Gramm-Rudman-Hollings, we expect to claim a zero budget deficit. By then, the calculation will include, not $63 billion, but $99 billion of the year's surplus Social Security revenues. If Congress continues to hold the budget deficit at zero, and continues to "lend and spend" excess Social Security revenues on non-Social Security programs, we will simply add the growing Social Security debt to the existing $2.3 trillion national debt. Within a decade, we would double the national debt to around $5 trillion.

And with this tremendous increase in debt will come a huge growth in annual interest payments on the debt. We already use 28 percent of our non-Social Security revenues to make interest payments on our Federal debt. If we continue to permit the national debt to grow by the process I have just described, our annual interest payments will more than double— from $177 billion to $375 billion—in just a decade. By the year 2000, depending on economic assumptions, as much as 60 percent of all non-Social Security revenues would be required to make interest payments alone. That is what I call *really* mortgaging the future. Eventually, we will be a nation so caught up in paying interest for the spending of this generation that we will have little revenue left to guard our shores or educate our children. I submit it is bad policy to divert our education, welfare, or defense resources in the first place. I also believe it is terrible politics to divert them in the form of interest payments to wealthy or foreign bondholders.

The dynamics of debt doubling are not only ominous for the Federal budget and in human terms, they also create some real vulnerabilities in our economy that cut close to our national security. The most troubling of these is our growing dependence on foreign lenders, brought on by a soaring debt and intensified by a declining private saving rate. The net saving rate in the United States has plummeted in the last ten years. Personal saving has dropped from more than 7 percent of disposable income to less than 4 percent in just six years. Were it not for private pensions, individual households would actually be net borrowers. At the same time, government deficits have risen from historical levels of about 1 to 2 percent of GNP to an average 5 percent of GNP in the 1980s. The combination has dropped net national saving from 6 percent of GNP in 1981 to only 2 percent in

1987. Almost all domestic personal saving is now being consumed by government deficits. In 1987, all but $13 billion of personal saving was offset by deficits. In that year, to meet the need for additional capital, we had to borrow $157 billion from abroad, largely from Japan. This is shocking because historically, and as recently as six years ago, we were net lenders to foreign countries.

Real Social Security saving—achieved by not lending and spending the annual addition to Social Security reserves—will be essential if we are ever to get our national saving rate back to the levels we knew in the 1970s. We must separate Social Security from the Gramm-Rudman-Hollings deficit targets and force ourselves to reduce all or part of the remaining deficit. At a minimum, we need to prevent Social Security's contribution to the budget from growing and casting an ever larger shadow over the deficit—at least until we reach Gramm-Rudman's zero deficit target in 1993. Then we can take the additional two or three years we will need to work the remaining Social Security surpluses out of the budget. This is the thrust of legislation I introduced last year as S. 2913, which I will reintroduce in the 101st Congress.

Truly removing Social Security from the budget will pay tremendous benefits. Among these is the attainment of "Truth-in-Budgeting" and the end of deficit deception. We would finally own up to what we really spend today and fully pay for it through general revenues. For tomorrow's retirees—the baby boom generation—the revenue we raise in the name of Social Security could then be available to pay a substantial part of their Social Security benefits rather than to pay for other programs and add to the national debt.

A second benefit of removing Social Security and controlling the national debt would be the greater flexibility we would give to future generations to meet their public program needs with their own resources. No longer would we be leveraging their incomes to pay for benefits and services we are consuming today. Instead, they would have the resources to meet their education, housing and health care needs.

But the most important benefit of creating a true Social Security reserve will be its contribution to real savings in the economy. If we eliminate the use of Social Security's funds to cover deficits, Social Security's reserves would be able to buy in and *replace* our $2.3 trillion of publicly held debt, rather than adding—by two times—a new burden on top of it. Finally, by freeing up private savings to meet our need for domestic investment capital, not only would we reduce our dependence on foreign capital, but we would substantially reduce the cost of capital to Americans and substantially increase our competitive posture in the world.

Over the next day you will be discussing many tough issues and a variety of options for treating Social Security's growing reserves. The fundamental reality we face in Social Security is that we will need to pay benefits to today's workers when they retire in twenty or thirty years. The costs will rise in this program with the baby boom generation's retirement, making today's concerns about surpluses a short-term phenomenon. In two or three decades we will be wrestling with deficits, and we will need additional revenues to pay Social Security's costs.

Economic growth is our key to success. With adequate growth we can pay those costs with no great added burden for tomorrow's workers. The more growth and productivity we have, the more manageable tomorrow's costs will be. Low inflation and interest rates and high real wages will keep the Government's costs down and revenues up. Doing something now to create additional saving to stimulate that growth will have the doubly satisfying result of making our problems more manageable and proving our economists and actuaries wrong.

As you begin discussing the various economic models and budgeting options we have to consider, I urge you to bear this in mind: Any policy that permits the open-ended lending and spending of Social Security's reserves will accelerate the increase in our massive national debt, further undermine our national saving and competitiveness, and commit a substantial portion of taxes paid by our grandchildren to interest payments. The handcuffing of future generations with unpaid debt and the involuntary diversion of their revenues to debt service will place an added burden on their workers—a burden that will make it harder for them to invest in human capital, meet the retirement costs of their time, and stimulate continued growth in the economy.

The best American minds in social insurance are here today, considering the most important social insurance topic. I will be very interested in hearing what conclusions you draw.

Setting Long-Run Deficit Reduction Targets: The Economics and Politics of Budget Design

Charles L. Schultze*

MORE THAN THIRTY YEARS AGO, RICHARD MUSGRAVE gave a powerful impetus to public finance analysis by distinguishing three major objectives of fiscal policy: resource allocation, income distribution, and economic stabilization.[1] Recent budgetary history and the current budget controversy suggest a fourth role for the budget—as a device for making intertemporal transfers, by increasing or decreasing the nation's saving rate. Musgrave only briefly discussed how the size of the budget balance could affect national saving and influence the allocation of national resources between consumption and investment, but the effects of the budget on the intergenerational distribution of resources are so central to the current budget controversy, that I think it useful to treat them as a separate objective. I shall suggest, in fact, that the influence of the budget on national saving should be a principal determinant of the targets we set for overall budget policy.

Until recently much of the policy discussion over the economic consequences of the budget deficit revolved around its effect on Musgrave's stabilization objective—how changes in the budget deficit affect aggregate demand. Some conservatives worried that the budget deficit would simply

---

*Director of Economic Studies, The Brookings Institution.

[1] Richard Musgrave, *The Theory of Public Finance*, McGraw-Hill, 1959, chapter 1, p. 5.

Author's Note: I have benefited greatly from discussions with Barry P. Bosworth, and from the book on Social Security which Bosworth and his co-authors, Henry Aaron and Gary Burtless, have recently completed. Unfortunately neither the discussion nor the book is guaranteed to have kept me from error.

lead to inflation; other conservatives, following Milton Friedman, dis-
counted the independent effect of deficits on aggregate demand and
inflation, but were afraid the deficits might generate inflation by encourag-
ing excess money creation to finance government borrowing. Liberals, on
the other hand, were concerned that the political force of the balanced
budget symbol would make it impossible to sustain high employment.

Thus, both liberals and conservatives supported changes in the budget
definition adopted in 1968 that for the first time *included* Social Security
revenues and expenditures in the overall (unified) budget. For purposes of
economic stabilization it was thought best to include *all* expenditures and
outlays in calculating the bottom line of the official budget, since all Federal
expenditures and outlays affect aggregate demand. Budget planners could
easily have operated with two sets of books, but given the political force of
the balanced budget symbol, it was deemed important that the public set of
books match the concept with which budget decisionmakers were most
concerned—and at the time, that was aggregate demand.

Attitudes about the budget deficit have changed in recent years: First,
like the prospect of hanging, $150 billion to $200 billion budget deficits tend
to concentrate the mind wonderfully. Reasonable people might quarrel
about whether a balanced budget or a $50 billion deficit was consistent
with a high employment but noninflationary path of aggregate demand.
Few believe that deficits of today's size are a necessary condition of high
employment. Second, even economists and politicians normally thought to
retain Keynesian leanings, place greater trust now than in the past on the
efficacy of monetary policy in offsetting at least moderate year-to-year
changes in fiscal policy. Several reasons account for this change. First,
consider the economic history of the last six years. Once the inflation of
the 1970s had receded, the Federal Reserve showed a great capacity for
keeping aggregate demand on a path that sustained economic growth with
low inflation. It performed this feat despite huge increases in the budget
deficit, massive swings in exchange rates, and a stock market crash second
only to 1929. Moreover, the Federal Reserve of the 1980s appears to have
won for itself much greater political freedom than it possessed in the 1950s,
1960s, and 1970s to permit, encourage, and engineer interest rate changes
sufficiently large to offset the aggregate demand effects of alterations in the
budget deficit (or other sources of demand instability). Finally, the growing
integration of world capital markets and the shift to floating exchange rates
have substantially increased the power of monetary policy to influence
aggregate demand, through its influence on the export and import-
competing sectors of the economy.

And so, I believe, it is appropriate to give much higher priority to the
national saving rate and intertemporal transfers and less priority to the

stabilization objective in setting budget deficit targets. This shift of emphasis does not imply that the new priorities take absolute precedence. First, there is a widely held (but not really well-documented) belief that annual reductions in the budget deficit of more than $35 billion to $40 billion might strain the ability of other parts of the economy to respond fast enough to avoid recession, even with highly competent and responsible monetary policy. In the unlikely event that the international exchange value of the dollar became firmly stuck at too high a level, large deficit reductions might create the problem of deficient aggregate demand, even with a relaxed monetary policy. Second, the fact that the current large budget deficits could probably be eliminated gradually without major aggregate demand problems does not of itself guarantee that enough domestic and foreign investment could be generated to run a large consolidated budget *surplus*, equal, for example, to the combined surplus in the Social Security trust funds and an actuarially strengthened Medicare trust fund (perhaps 2-½ percent of GNP by the mid-1990s). I will return to this question later. First, I want to examine the political and economic aspects of setting deficit targets principally in terms of national saving objectives. I shall assume that a reasonably wide range of alternatives would be consistent with the stabilization goal.

Social Security, the Budget, and the National Saving Rate

Starting early in the next century, as the current baby boom generation begins to retire, the number of retirees collecting Social Security benefits will rise sharply relative to the number of workers making payroll contributions to the Social Security system. Under a "pay-as-you-go" system of financing, with taxes set to match current benefit payments, the next generation of workers would face a sharply increased burden of taxation to support the system.

In 1978 and 1983 Congress restructured the nation's Social Security (OASDI) system so that the current baby boom generation of workers will pay enough taxes approximately to finance its own Social Security retirement benefits. The tax schedule was set high enough to ensure that the Social Security trust funds will run increasing surpluses through the rest of this century and into the next, in order to accumulate funds and invest in assets to help pay future benefits.[2] In 1988 the Social Security trust funds

---

[2] If, regularly—say every five years—tax rates were appropriately adjusted, the system could continue to be one in which each generation paid its own way.

had an excess of revenues over expenditures of \$40 billion; by 1994 that annual surplus will mount to about \$110 billion. Other retirement trust funds in the U.S. budget—Medicare, Civil Service Retirement, and Military Retirement—are also running annual surpluses. The total annual accumulation in all these retirement trust funds is shown below:[3]

	($ billions)		
	1989	1990	1994
Social Security	52	63	113
Other Retirement	57	56	62
Total	109	119	175

Although the Hospital Insurance Fund is now running a modest annual surplus, currently legislated tax rates are far below those necessary to pay for currently promised benefits. The tax rate, and hence the annual surplus necessary to enable the current working generation to finance its own cash and medical retirement costs, would thus be larger than shown above.

The mere accumulation of financial assets in social insurance trust funds does not, of course, mean that one generation is financing its own retirement and relieving the next of any burden. The consumption of each generation of retirees must come out of the income and wealth of the then current economy. Thus, if this generation is to finance its own retirement, the nation as a whole must now add to its aggregate saving, accumulate productive wealth, and raise production of the next generation so that the consumption of retirees is not a burden on that generation.[4] But if surpluses in the Social Security and other retirement funds are used to justify deficits

---

[3] Congressional Budget Office, *The Economic and Budget Outlook, An Update*, August 1988, Table II-5, p. 60.

[4] One should be very careful about arguing that an appropriate current increase in national saving will ease or eliminate the burden of a large retired population on the then working generation. Whatever we now do by way of taxing ourselves to put away additional saving, as represented by a surplus in the Social Security fund, the next working generation will have to devote a *larger fraction* of its national income to paying retirement benefits than is now the case. What a current increase in saving and productive investment can do is to raise the future *level* of productivity and income. The higher proportion of income going to the retired will then be taken from a higher national income. But by, say, the third decade of the twenty-first century, no one except a few economic historians will realize that national income at the time is higher because workers in the last decade of the prior century and the first two decades of the next one increased saving. From a social and political standpoint, an increase in the "burden" of Social Security will appear to be occurring. (I am indebted to George Perry for this point.)

in the rest of the Federal budget, national saving and wealth accumulation will not have been increased.

While the purpose of pre-funding the retirement funds can only be met if the annual surpluses are added to the national saving that would otherwise take place, this conclusion does not tell us what the overall saving rate ought to be or what should be the balance, positive or negative, in the government budget outside the retirement funds. To examine these questions, it is useful to start with a brief review of the course of national saving in the postwar era.

The Postwar History of the National Saving Rate

Table 1 presents the basic data on the national saving rate since 1956. Private and government saving are expressed as a percent of net national product (national income at market prices). Private saving is the sum of personal saving and retained corporate earnings. The data are cyclically adjusted, since the federal deficit as a share of national saving varies substantially with the rate of unemployment.[5] The growing annual surpluses in state and local pension funds for municipal employees have been reclassified from the government to the private sector, since employee pension funds in the private sector are treated as part of personal saving.[6] State and local budget surpluses or deficits, excluding pension funds, are included in the government sector. Their impact is small because they have been very close to balance, on average, over the period covered by Table 1. (They averaged a deficit of 0.2 percent of NNP.) In the discussion that follows, I therefore treat the public sector deficit and the federal deficit as synonymous.

---

[5] Private and government saving rates were regressed against DNAIRU, a term representing the excess of the actual unemployment rate over the rate of unemployment estimated by the CBO to be consistent with a stable inflation rate (*The Economic and Budget Outlook, Fiscal Years 1989–1993*, Table B-2). Private saving showed no consistent cyclical pattern. Government saving was, of course, cyclically sensitive. The government deficit was adjusted to "high employment" levels using the coefficient on DNAIRU and combined with private saving (unadjusted) to produce a cyclically adjusted total saving rate. The equation from which the coefficient on government saving was derived was fit from 1956 to 1980; common time trend on DNAIRU and GSAV/NNP after 1980 biased the DNAIRU coefficient upward when the equation was fit through 1987.

[6] State and local accumulation in social insurance funds was shifted out of the government sector to the private sector. That is not exactly the appropriate adjustment, since a small part of that accumulation does not represent pension fund accumulation, but the resulting error is small.

Table 1
National Savings, Cyclically Adjusted,
as Percent of Net National Product, 1956–87[a]

Year	Net Saving	Private	Government
	Annual Data		
1956	9.3	9.1	0.2
1957	8.2	9.0	−0.8
1958	6.6	8.7	−2.1
1959	8.2	8.8	−0.5
1960	8.3	7.9	0.4
1961	8.3	8.5	−0.3
1962	8.2	9.2	−1.0
1963	8.7	8.9	−0.2
1964	8.9	10.1	−1.2
1965	9.4	10.7	−1.2
1966	8.3	10.3	−2.1
1967	7.0	10.8	−3.8
1968	6.5	9.4	−2.9
1969	7.2	8.3	−1.1
1970	6.6	8.9	−2.3
1971	7.5	10.0	−2.5
1972	8.2	9.4	−1.2
1973	10.1	10.9	−0.8
1974	8.2	9.6	−1.3
1975	7.2	10.8	−3.6
1976	7.7	9.8	−2.1
1977	8.3	9.6	−1.3
1978	9.0	9.9	−0.9
1979	8.5	9.1	−0.6

The U.S. national saving rate collapsed in the 1980s. From an average of close to 8 percent of national income in the 1950s, 1960s, and 1970s it plummeted during the 1980s and is now only 2.5 to 3 percent of income. The third panel in Table 1 shows ten-year averages of cyclically adjusted data excluding large deficits related to the Vietnam War and major reces-

Table 1 (cont.)
National Savings, Cyclically Adjusted, as Percent of Net National Product, 1956–87[a]

Year	Net Saving	Private	Government
Annual Data			
1980	6.7	8.3	– 1.6
1981	7.6	8.6	– 1.0
1982	5.1	7.6	– 2.5
1983	4.9	7.9	– 3.0
1984	5.8	9.0	– 3.2
1985	3.7	7.8	– 4.1
1986	3.0	7.4	– 4.4
1987	2.3	6.1	– 3.8
Ten-Year Averages			
1956–60	8.1	8.7	– 0.6
1961–70	7.9	9.5	– 1.6
1971–80	8.1	9.7	– 1.6
1981–86	5.0	8.1	– 3.0
1987–88[b]	2.5	6.4	– 3.8
Averages less Recession and War Years[c]			
1956–60	8.1	8.7	– 0.6
1961–70	8.4	9.4	– 1.0
1971–80	8.4	9.5	– 1.1
1981–86	5.0	8.2	– 3.2
1987–88[b]	2.5	6.4	– 3.8

[a] See text, footnote 5, for explanation of cyclical adjustment.
[b] Weighted average of 1987 and the first three quarters of 1988.
[c] Recession and war years: 1967, 1968, 1970, 1971, 1975, 1976, 1982, and 1983.
Source: U.S. Bureau of Economic Analysis, *National Income and Product Accounts.*

sions (when tax cuts or spending increases temporarily raised even cyclically adjusted budget deficits). In the 1950s, 1960s, and 1970s, national saving averaged just over 8 percent of net national product (NNP), with private saving averaging a little more than 9 percent offset by a government budget deficit of slightly above 1 percent. National saving has since fallen to less than 3 percent of NNP in 1987. The drop of more than 5 percentage points was about equally split between declines in private and in public saving.

The Determinants of National Saving

The decline in the national saving rate and its components raises two issues: First, to what extent do changes in government saving generate changes in national saving and to what extent do they lead to offsetting changes in private saving? Second, to what extent can transitory factors, which might be expected to reverse themselves, explain the recent decline in private saving?

Ten years ago I would have answered the first questions by showing how the national saving rate has declined in recent years and how an elimination of the federal budget deficit, and perhaps its conversion to a surplus, could change the saving rate. I would not have thought it necessary to argue that in periods of high employment a change in the budget surplus or deficit would have no effect on national saving. But now, at least in academic circles, one is forced to deal with the following hypothesis, allegedly originated by David Ricardo and popularized by Robert Barro: taxpaying consumers act as infinitely farsighted and generationally altruistic households, whose savings plans are continuously adapted to maintain generation-spanning wealth objectives in the face of current changes in government fiscal policies. According to this line of reasoning, a personal tax cut that produces a budget deficit will cause households to calculate that for them or their descendants future taxes will have to rise and disposable incomes will fall. They will, therefore, save the whole tax cut in order to preserve the pattern of consumption they had previously chosen for themselves and their heirs.[7]

I put little credence in this hypothesis. Changes in the government budget do change national saving. The empirical studies provide overwhelming evidence against the Ricardo-Barro hypothesis.[8] On a more informal basis, the fact that the recent large budget deficits coincide with a *fall*, rather than a *rise*, in private saving would seem flatly to contradict the Barro-Ricardo view. Nevertheless, advocates of this view argue that other

[7] This argument omits the distorting effects of taxes on private decisions but for purposes of this analysis we can safely ignore them.

[8] For a summary, see Douglas Bernheim, "Ricardian Equivalence: An Evaluation of Theory and Evidence," *NBER Macroeconomics Annual*, vol. 2, 1987, pp. 263–304. See also Lawrence Summers and Chris Carroll, "Why Is U.S. National Saving So Low?" *Brookings Papers on Economic Activity*, 2:1987, pp. 607–17, and Summers, "Issues in National Savings Policy," *NBER Working Paper #1710*, September 1985.

factors may have independently depressed the private saving rate (for example, large capital gains in common stocks and housing may have encouraged consumption), and that the private saving rate might have tumbled more than it did, had it not been for the saving-inducing effect of the budget deficits.

Lawrence Summers and Chris Carroll recently examined and disposed of the capital gains issue.[9] However, since one cannot establish long-term targets for the proper balance in the budget as a means of affecting the national saving rate without considering what is likely to happen to private saving, I have myself tried to determine whether the recent collapse in the private saving rate has been driven by events likely to reverse themselves or by long-term trends.

Both the personal and the corporate saving rates have fallen in recent years. I fit the following equation to explain the personal saving rate:

(1) S/Y_d = F (SFG, SFG(-1), SC, LSPRES, DYDR, T, T75)

where:

S/Y_d = personal saving including state and local pension funds (S) divided by disposable income, Y_d.

SFG = cyclically adjusted government budget surplus ($+$) or deficit ($-$) as a share of net national product (NNP). SFG(-1) is the value of SFG for the proceeding period.

SC = corporate retained earnings as a share of NNP.

LSPRES = residual from a regression of the natural logarithm (multiplied by 100) of the deflated Standard & Poor's stock price index against SC. The coefficient on this variable indicates the effect on personal saving of changes in real stock prices other than those associated with changes in retained corporate earnings. One-third of the variance in corporate earnings stock prices between 1956 and 1987 can be explained by variations in corporate earnings; the remaining two-thirds is included in this variable.

DYDR = annual percent change in real disposable income.

T = time trend, a variable with a value of 1 in 1957, 2 in 1958 and so on.

T75 = a time trend starting in 1975. The trend value for years after 1975 is the sum of the coefficients on the two trend terms.

---

9 Summers and Carroll, pp. 613–14.

Table 2
Regression Equation Explaining the Adjusted Personal Saving Rate[a]

	1956–80	1956–87
Constant	7.43 (11.1)	7.59 (12.5)
T	.14 (5.0)	.14 (6.4)
T75[b]	−.50 (4.1)	−.47 (11.4)
SFG	−.43 (3.7)	−.36 (3.5)
SFG(−1)	.30 (2.5)	.27 (2.3)
SC	−.74 (3.8)	−.79 (4.5)
LSPRES	−.02 (2.3)	−.02 (3.0)
DYDR	.19 (2.2)	.21 (2.8)
$\overline{R}^2$	.79	.84
D.W.	1.70	1.77

[a] See text for definitions of variables; t statistics in parentheses.

[b] Time trend beginning with 1 in 1975; the net trend for years after 1974 is equal to the *sum* of coefficients on T and T75.

Except as noted, all variables are expressed in percentage points.

This equation allows for the influence of the cyclically adjusted government budget deficit (SFG) and corporate retained earnings (SC) on the personal saving rate. The coefficients on those variables should tell us the extent to which individuals see through the corporate and government "veils." The income change variable, DYDR, captures the income-averaging phenomenon—as income initially increases (decreases), consumption adjusts sluggishly and saving is temporarily higher (lower). LSPRES captures the effect on saving behavior of stock market capital gains over and above those associated with changes in retained earnings (SC). The time variables allow for a trend in the personal saving rate and particularly for a downtrend in recent years not associated with other identifiable causes.

Table 2 gives the results of fitting equation (1) for two periods: 1956–80 and 1956–87. And Figure 1 shows the errors in forecast seven years out of sample, using the coefficients from the 1956–80 fit to forecast the results from 1981–87 (including a continuation of the downward time trend that began in 1975). As is clear from Table 2, the coefficients are virtually the same in the two periods. The results presented in the figure show that the equation estimated on data from 1956 through 1980 accurately tracks the recent fall in the saving rate; indeed, its 1987 error was in predicting a saving rate even lower than the actual one. The downtrend in the personal saving rate from 1975 to 1980 continued at approximately that same rate thereafter

(Although the patterns of forecast errors in the last several years' downtrend may conceivably have halted after 1985).

Several other results stand out, based on the equation estimated on data for the period 1956 through 1987: First, a change in the cyclically adjusted budget deficit of $1 does lead initially to an offsetting change in adjusted personal saving of about 29 cents. (SFG is the ratio of the budget surplus to net national product; the dependent variable, S/Y_d, is the personal saving rate out of disposable income, which averages 80 percent of net national product. Thus, the immediate effect of a $1 change in SFG on the percent of the personal saving rate is $.8 \times -.36 = -.29$.) But this phenomenon is transitory. If the shift in the budget persists, the offsetting change in private saving drops to only 7 cents. Thus, a $1 increase in the government deficit leads, after a year, to a drop in national saving of about 93 cents. Assuming

Figure 1
Adjusted Personal Saving Rate:
Actual, Estimate, and Forecast
(Percent of Disposable Personal Income)

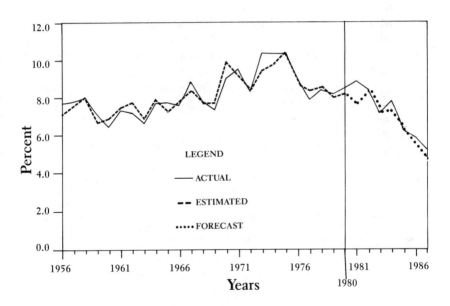

Saving adjusted to include surplus of state and local insurance funds. 1981–87 forecast from regression equations fit to 1956–1980. See text.

Source: U.S. Bureau of Economic Analysis, *National Income and Product Accounts.*

that business saving is not directly affected by the government deficit, the Barro-Ricardo effect is worth a paltry 7 cents on the dollar.

Second, when planning their saving objectives, households apparently do take into account changes in the retained earnings of corporations whose stock they own. Personal saving falls 63 cents for each $1 increase in corporate saving.[10]

Third, appreciation of stock prices beyond what can be explained by the change in retained corporate earnings accounts for only a modest part of the decline in personal saving. From 1975 to 1982 such changes in stock prices explain none of the 1.9 percentage point fall in the adjusted personal saving rate. Of the further 3.3 percentage point decline in the saving rate that occurred from 1982 to 1987, only 0.9 percentage points can be attributed to the stock market rise.[11]

Fourth, the coefficient on a variable measuring the volume of real capital gains accruing to households from residential structures and real estate, as a ratio to real disposable income, had the "wrong" (positive) sign, and was insignificant. I dropped it from the version of the equation shown in Table 2.

Demographic variables add nothing to the equation. Table 3 shows the ratio of the supposedly "high saving" population, ages 35 to 59, to the adult working-age population. Just as the personal saving rate was falling fastest, after 1981, this ratio ceased its earlier decline and began rising. Not surprisingly, when added to the equation its coefficient is negative. Those who argue that the private saving rate will shortly be increasing because of "favorable" demographic changes are likely to be disappointed.[12]

The equation confirms what the eye picks up—there has been a downward trend in personal saving since 1975. Neither financial variables, such

---

[10] This result is derived from the coefficient on SC by the transformation (.8 × −.79 = −.63).

[11] It can be shown that relative size of the coefficients on SC and LSPRES in equation (1), together with the coefficient on SC in the auxiliary equation used to derive LSPRES, implies that stock price fluctuations associated with actual changes in retained earnings exert almost three times as much influence on the personal saving rate as do stock price fluctuations stemming from other sources (and there may be some downward bias in the statistical estimate of this 3 to 1 ratio).

[12] A variable representing the ratio of residential construction to disposable income, lagged over several years, improves the fit of the equation (raising the R^2 from 0.84 to 0.90) and modestly raises the Barro-Ricardo coefficients, the sum of SFG and SFG (−1), to −0.32. The rationale for its inclusion is that decisions to invest in housing lead to "forced" saving in the later years. However, the resulting variable is unsatisfactory; in particular, it performs poorly out of sample. When fit on data from 1956 through 1980, the root mean square error of the out-of-sample forecasting errors for 1987 are almost twice those of the equation in Table 3. The reason appears to be that residential construction is strongly correlated with the government budget deficit in the first part

Table 3
Share of "High Saving" Age Group in Working-Age Population
(percent)

	(Age 35–59) / (Age 20–65)
1956–60	55.6
1961–65	56.4
1966–70	54.0
1971–75	50.1
1976–80	47.3
1981	45.9
1982	46.3
1983	46.5
1984	46.7
1985	46.9
1986	47.4
1987	48.0

Source: U.S. Bureau of the Census.

as capital gains on stock and real estate, nor demographic variables explain this trend.

With no structural explanation for the post-1975 drop in the personal saving rate one cannot be certain about future saving rates. Nevertheless, I conclude that, in the absence of some positive indication that saving rates will rise, it would be prudent to assume that the adjusted personal saving rate will not substantially increase above its recent (1988) level of 6 percent of disposable income (slightly under 5 percent of NNP). With business saving running at 2 percent of NNP, this yields a projected net private saving rate of 6.5 to 7 percent of NNP. Virtually all of a budget deficit reduction would show up as an increase in national saving and would not, except for a brief transition period, be offset by a reduction in private saving.

---

of the period but not significantly so in recent years. Thus, when the residential variable is included, the coefficients on GSF sum to −0.74 in the 1956–80 period but fall to −0.32 when the period of fit is changed to 1956–87 and to −0.12 when the period is again changed to 1963–87. I did not retain this variable in the final version of the equation. In any event, when it is included the estimated downward trend in personal saving from 1975 on is virtually unchanged from that reported in Table 3.

Deficit Targets and National Saving Objectives

To the extent that long-term deficit targets are set to achieve some national saving objective, the initial question to be asked is: "What national saving and investment rate is needed to sustain the current growth of national productivity and equip a growing labor force with the requisite capital stock, assuming no continuing reliance on the import of saving from abroad (that is, a zero current account balance)?" The current growth of productivity may not be optimal, but it is a good place to start in deciding what Federal budget deficit or surplus, combined with private saving, will generate a level of national saving that is at least minimally satisfactory.

Table 4 sets forth some simple relationships between the growth of national output, the growth of the private capital stock, and the rate of national saving, historically and projected over the period between 1988 and the year 2000. It starts from the identity:

$$(2)\ s_n = i_f + i_v + i_o$$

where s_n = net national saving, i_f = net fixed investment, i_v = inventory investment, and i_o = net foreign investment (which, when negative, represents an inflow of foreign saving into the United States). In current dollars, the net fixed investment share (i_f) is equal to the growth in the capital stock ($\dot{k}$) times the capital-output ratio (k/q) times the ratio of the price of capital goods, to the price of other goods (P_k/P_q).

$$(3)\ i_f = \dot{k} \times (k/q) \times P_k/P_q)$$

The growth of the capital stock, $\dot{k}$, is equal to the growth of employment plus the growth in the amount of capital per worker:

$$(4)\ \dot{k} = \dot{n} + (\dot{k/n}),$$

where $\dot{n}$ is the growth rate of employment and $(\dot{k/n})$ is the growth rate of capital per worker.

From 1988 through 2000 the labor force and employment are projected to grow more slowly than in earlier years, and so on this account the capital stock may be expected to grow more slowly. But what about the growth of capital per worker? Historically the U.S. capital stock has grown more rapidly than the labor force. A rapidly rising ratio of capital per worker raises output per worker and total output, but depresses the rate of return to investment. Advances in technology, improvements in worker skills, and other productivity-enhancing developments, called multifactor productivity growth, raise the rate of return. Thus, the faster multifactor productivity grows, the more rapidly capital per worker can increase with-

Table 4
Saving, Investment, and Growth

| | Annual Growth Rates[a] | | | Average | National Saving and Its Uses[b] | | | |
| | | | | | | | Uses | |
	Potential net output[c]	Net capital	Potential employment[c]	capital-output ratio[b]	National saving rate	Net fixed capital investment	Inventory change	Foreign investment
Actual:								
1956–79	3.4	3.6	1.7	1.94	8.2	6.7	0.9	0.5
1979–87	2.6	2.6	1.7	2.02	4.1	5.2	0.4	–1.5
Projected:[d]								
1988–2000	2.2	2.3	1.2	2.09	5.3	4.5	0.8	0.0

[a] The output, capital, and employment data pertain to the private domestic sector.

[b] To use this ratio to derive the national saving rate consistent with any given growth of the capital stock, the relevant output concept is total net national product.

[c] Historical growth rates of potential net output and employment are derived from Congressional Budget Office estimates of potential GNP and the nonaccelerating inflation rate of unemployment, in *The Economic and Budget Outlook, Fiscal Years 1989–93*, (Feb. 1988), Table B-2.

[d] The projection incorporates the following additional assumptions:
1. The projected growth of potential output is based on an average annual rise in private employment of 1.1 percent (based on BLS labor force projections), and a somewhat optimistic assumption that the "high employment" unemployment rate falls from 5.7 percent in 1987 to 5 percent by 2000.
2. The private capital stock is assumed to grow 0.1 percent a year faster than potential output, implying a very slight downward pressure on rates of return. Because the capital-labor ratio is projected to grow a little faster than in the 1979–87 period, projected output per worker rises a shade faster than it did in those years (1.0 versus 0.9 percent).
3. Inventory investment as a share of NNP is projected to be just a little below its historic ratio.

Source: U.S. Bureau of Economic Analysis, *National Income and Product Accounts*.

out depressing the profitability of investment.[13] Alternatively, a rise in the
capital-labor ratio sufficiently fast relative to the advance of technology will
cause the capital stock to grow faster than output and the rate of return to
fall.[14] As shown by the data in Table 4, the capital-output ratio in the United
States has risen slightly during most of the postwar period. The rate of
return has fallen slightly (not shown in Table 4).

The rate of multifactor productivity growth fell from 1.9 percent in
1956–73 to 0.8 percent in the period since 1979, and no evidence is available
that suggests this latest rate of growth will improve in the years ahead. The
growth of the labor force between 1988 and 2000 is also lower than it has
been in recent years. Thus, in the absence of any improvement in multifactor productivity growth, the rate of growth in national output, and the rate
of growth in the capital stock consistent with avoiding any major decrease
in the rate of return to capital, will be lower in the years ahead than in
earlier postwar years.

Before I project the national saving rate "required" to maintain capital's
contribution to the rate of productivity growth, one major problem has to
be dealt with. In calculating the *real* value of investment in computers and
related equipment, the producers of the official national income accounts
now deflate the sales of those goods by a hedonic price index. It counts as
price decreases the very rapid annual improvements in the speed and other
characteristics of computers. The aggregate measures of real investment
and of real GNP and NNP are the equivalent of quantities weighted by
1982 prices. Since computers constitute a significant fraction of business
investment, and since the estimated price of computers is now falling
rapidly compared to the price of other investment goods, this approach has
the effect of substantially raising the estimated magnitude of *real* private
investment as a share of *real* NNP relative to its current dollar share of
current dollar NNP. Since the 1982 relative price of computers, used as a
weight to get the quantity index, was twice the current relative price — and
the price is falling steadily—the problem keeps growing. The table at right,

---

[13] The relationships are given by the following equation:

$$\dot{\Pi}_k = \dot{mpk} = \lambda - S_l(\dot{k} - \dot{n})$$

where Π_k is the rate of return to capital (the marginal product of capital, mpk)
λ = the rate of multifactor productivity growth
S_l = labor's share of national income
$\dot{k}, \dot{n}$ = the rates of growth of capital and labor, respectively
This formulation assumes a Cobb-Douglas production function with an elasticity of
substitution between capital and labor of 1. If that elasticity, σ, is different from 1, the
coefficient of the change in the capital-labor ratio, $(\dot{k} - \dot{n})$, becomes S_l/σ.

[14] Again, given a Cobb-Douglas production function.

relating to net private fixed investment, gives some sense of the magnitudes:

| | Fixed Investment/NNP | | |
	Current $	1982 $	Relative Price of Investment Goods
1956	7.7	7.7	1.00
1979	7.7	7.9	0.97
1987	4.8	5.3	0.90

On one measure—its share in 1982 dollars—net fixed investment has dropped 28 percent since 1979. By the current dollar measure, the share has dropped by 43 percent.

If the new technique for measuring the output of the computer industry accurately reflects the increasing contribution of a dollar's worth of computer purchases to national output, then a dollar's worth of national resources that are saved now can produce more investment goods than in the past. The rapid pace of technological advance within the computer and related industries acts as a capital-saving innovation—our saving has shrunk, but what remains is more productive. And if the relative price of capital goods should keep falling, we could maintain the real investment share at a steadily declining saving rate.

If the rapid growth of computer "capital," generated by the new measurement technique, were purely a statistical artifact, so that the "true" growth of the productive capital stock were being substantially overstated by the official estimates of investment, then everything else being equal, the reported capital-output ratio should have risen sharply. That did not happen. In the past several years the capital-output ratio rose, after some years of decline, but not very rapidly, and no more than in the years before 1980. But since we do not know, even within fairly wide limits, what change in the capital-output ratio is normal, this fact is anything but conclusive.[15] The relative decline in the price of fixed investment goods has been slowing in the last several years. For the purpose of the projection I assumed that between now and the next century, the rate of decline would be half what it has been in those recent years.

The last line in Table 4 projects the national saving rate that would be required, *in the absence of any further inflow of capital from abroad,* to

---

[15] We could observe the residual in a production function using two different capital stock measures—with and without the hedonic price correction for computers—but that would not tell us much since we have no way of knowing which residual most closely approximates real world events.

maintain roughly the "status quo" with respect to the contribution of capital to the growth of national productivity. The projection assumes that growth of multifactor productivity continues at its 1979–87 pace. The projected national saving rate of 5.3 percent between 1988 and 2000 would support capital investment sufficient to equip the growing labor force and to increase the capital stock per worker at a pace that slightly depresses the rate of return to capital and slightly increases the capital-output ratio, as was the case in most of the postwar era.

Under the stated assumptions, a 5.3 percent national saving rate would maintain the growth of potential output per worker at its trend rate of growth (1 percent a year). The amount of investment that has to be financed by that saving is a little lower than in the past few years because the growth of the labor force is lower. And the saving rate can ease down a little beyond that because of the favorable relative price movement for capital goods.

Earlier in the paper I argued that there were no solid reasons to expect the private saving rate to rise significantly above its current rate of 6.5 to 7 percent of NNP. Should the cyclically adjusted government deficit duplicate its pre-1980 historic average—between 1 and 1.5 percent of NNP (depending on whether one includes or excludes the Vietnam War years and the recessions of the 1970s), the net national saving rate would then lie in the 5 to 5.5 percent range, or about what would be "required" to maintain the currently estimated growth of economic potential over the next decade. The historical, projected, and "required" saving rates are as follows:

| | **(Percent of NNP)** | | |
	Net Saving	**Private**	**Government**
Historical: 1956–79	8	9.5	−1 to −1.5
Hypothetical Projection	5 to 5.5	6.5 to 7	−1 to −1.5
"Required," 1988–2000	5.3		

There is nothing necessarily optimal about the projected saving rate. Given the expected growth of the labor force and the recent pace of multifactor productivity growth, it simply would enable the nation to support a level of investment sufficient to maintain, and indeed slightly increase, growth in output per worker without continued reliance on overseas borrowing. Like the national saving rate of the 1956–79 base period, the projected saving rate would keep the nation's domestic capital stock growing just a little faster than output, slightly depressing the rate of return to capital. In the 1956–79 period, however, our national saving rate not only achieved that goal but also supported overseas investment of an average of 0.5 percent of NNP per year. The projected saving rate will not do that. Based on almost three decades of actual public and private saving decisions, rather than on optimal saving and growth rules, one could make a good case that the projected national saving rate is too low because it does not allow for any foreign investment. It would surely be difficult to argue that the projected saving rate is too high, but it can, conservatively, be used as a *minimum* baseline. To this baseline should then be added the extra national saving required to meet the next century's retirement bulge, which the growing surpluses in the Social Security trust fund represent.

Comparison of Baseline Saving "Requirements" and Availability

Saving Requirements:	Percent of NNP
• Minimum baseline (maintain current productivity growth)	5.3
Saving Availability:	
• Private saving	6.5 to 7.0
• Budget deficit consistent with meeting above requirement	− 1.2 to − 1.7

Additional Saving for the Next Century's Retirement Bulge

The Social Security amendments of 1977 and 1983 will result in large trust fund reserves. The annual surpluses in the Social Security trust funds that will generate these reserves can only be translated into economic reality if they are used to increase national saving and the stock of national wealth, thereby boosting future national output and income above what would otherwise have occurred. In practical terms this means that national saving ought to be increased above the baseline level projected above.

By 1994 the annual Social Security surplus will amount to 1.8 percent of net national product. Added to the baseline national saving rate, this reserve accumulation gives a savings requirement of 7.1 percent of NNP (5.3 + 1.8). Further addition of the annual surplus in the Medicare trust fund, as now projected, raises the total trust fund surplus to 2.1 percent and the required national saving rate to 7.4 percent. The Medicare tax rate, however, is much below that necessary to pay for the projected cost of currently promised benefits. While I do not know by how much the introduction of an adequate tax rate would raise the annual surplus by 1994, it would surely add at least another 0.4 percent of NNP to the annual accumulation, further increasing the combined trust fund surpluses to 2.5 percent and the required national saving rate to 7.8 percent.

After inclusion of the additional saving needs generated by demographic developments and measured by the surplus in the government retirement funds, national saving availability and requirements compare as follows:

Saving Requirements:	Percent of NNP
• Maintain potential growth at recent levels	5.3
• Add Social Security "saving"	2.5
Total	7.8
Saving Availability:	
• Private saving	6.5 to 7
• **Additional saving required:**	0.8 to 1.3

This admittedly crude exercise suggests that an *overall* budget surplus of about 1 percent of NNP might be a reasonable long-run goal. The table below contrasts saving and investment in 1987 (as a share of NNP) with the situation that would prevail if the above national saving target were reached by 1994:

	1987	1994
Net national saving	2.0	7.8
Overseas borrowing (negative net foreign investment)	4.0	0
Net domestic investment	5.8[a]	7.8

[a] Net domestic investment differs from the sum of net national saving and overseas borrowing by the amount of the statistical discrepancy in the national income accounts.

An overall budget surplus of 1 percent of NNP implies the following budget targets for 1994:

	Budget Targets, 1994 Percent of NNP	$ billion
1. Budget defined to include retirement trust funds	+1	+ 65
2. Budget defined to exclude retirement trust funds		
• trust funds	+2.5	+160
• other accounts	−1.5	− 95

The precision of these estimates is, of course, spurious, but they do indicate the general magnitudes of reasonable targets.

Some Reasons to Aim for a More Ambitious Target

Although the raw calculations suggest that the budget excluding the Social Security trust funds need not be fully in balance, I think that a mixture of political and economic reasons argues that the nation set a target for a balanced budget, defined to exclude the Social Security trust funds. First, my estimates of saving requirements are based on the average for the period 1988–2000, using 1994 as a convenient midpoint. Under the best of conditions, however, a budget surplus will not be reached by 1994. The target budget surplus for the late 1990s should be larger than the 1 percent level not only to make up for some of the "required" saving lost before 1994 but also because additions to the retirement fund reserves will continue growing past 1994. Second, even if we exclude years of recession and war, the average budget deficit from 1956 through 1980 was 1.1 percent of NNP. Thus, if we set a target of balancing the budget (defined to exclude Social Security and Medicare trust funds), we might in fact succeed in reducing the budget deficit to a modest 1 to 1.5 percent of NNP. Finally, I have made no references to the trust funds for civilian and military retirees, but they are running surpluses which, in principle, should be added to the national saving target.

Can America Find Enough Investment Opportunities?

The national saving rate can be increased to 7.8 percent compared to the 5.3 percent "status quo" projections only if outlets are found in the form of domestic or foreign investments. While the baseline investment projection implies a tiny decline in the rate of return to capital over the projection period, increasing domestic investment by an additional 2.3 percent of NNP would drive down the marginal product of capital and the rate of return more substantially.

Period	Percent Decline In the Rate of Return
1956–73	– 1.5
1973–87	– 1.5
Projected:	
1988–2000: A: 5.3 percent saving rate	– 1.5
B: 7.7 percent saving rate	–14.0

Note that the changes are in *percents*, not *percentage points*. Thus, if the net (before tax) profit rate on invested capital is now 12 percent, a 1.5 percent decline would take it to 11.8 percent and a 14 percent decline to 10.3 percent by the year 2000.

The fall of 1.5 to 2 percentage points in the rate of return to capital that might occur if the national saving rate were raised to 7.7 percent is probably manageable; the cost of capital could easily fall enough to accommodate such a decline in the rate of return. On the other hand, the weight of recent evidence gives only a modest role to neoclassical cost-of-capital factors.[16] Over the past fifteen years the sharp rise in the average real

[16] See Peter K. Clark, "Investment in the 1970s: Theory Performance and Prediction," *Brookings Papers on Economic Activity*, 1:1979, pp. 73–124; Barry Bosworth, *Tax Incentives and Economic Growth*, Brookings (1984), pp. 98–111; and Patric H. Hendershott and Sheng-Ching Hu, "Investment in Producers Equipment," in *How Taxes Affect Economic Behavior*, Aaron and Pechman, eds., Brookings (1983), pp. 85–130.

interest rate has not had a major negative impact on investment. It might correspondingly be the case that even a substantial decline in real interest rates would not be sufficient to permit an absorption of the increased saving by domestic investment.

Nevertheless, the fall in the return to capital associated with the target saving rate is not so large as to preclude setting ambitious national saving goals. Long-term budget targets ought to be designed on the assumption that absorption will be possible. Since reaching the higher national saving goal will, unfortunately, be a long and gradual process, we will have plenty of time to discover the limits of the possible, without having to make a single grand commitment.

If domestic investment of all the added national saving proves troublesome, the United States could run a balance of payments surplus and invest abroad. This may prove difficult, however, because most other advanced industrial countries face a demographic future similar to ours. In some, most notably Japan, the increase in the proportion of the population that is elderly will be even more dramatic than it will be here. While many of these countries are on a pay-as-you-go system of Social Security financing, the prospective burden of future retirement benefits may push most of them to run fiscal surpluses as a means of increasing national saving rates.[17] In that case, the United States could invest large sums abroad only in the developing countries. Investments in developing countries carry serious default risks, but assuming cooperation with international institutions, it might be possible to invest significant amounts at realized rates of return that approximate those here at home.

In summary, it seems likely that the additional national saving represented by the Social Security and Medicare surpluses could be profitably invested either at home or abroad. Although the evidence is too tenuous for us to be certain of this conclusion, there is no need to make an inviolable commitment. The nation can set an ambitious saving target and have plenty of time to back off if investment, at home or abroad, is slow in responding to the lower cost of capital made possible by higher national saving rates.

Setting Budget Targets: Accounting Concepts and Political Symbols

At some abstract level of rationality, the design of a long-run budget policy ought not to be affected by how revenues and outlays are labeled or by how "the" budget deficit is defined. Suppose, for example, the President and the Congress agreed that the current and scheduled surpluses in the

---

[17] See OECD *Economic Outlook*, December 1987, Chart D, p. 20 and pp. 24-26.

Social Security funds ought to be used to increase national saving, and that the budget for the rest of government operations ought to be brought into balance by the mid 1990s. That goal could be achieved in either of two ways: 1) by including Social Security funds in the budget and aiming for an overall budget surplus equal to the surplus in the trust funds; or 2) by excluding the trust fund surplus from the budget and aiming at a balance in the budget so defined. Similarly, as long as the appropriate information on capital outlays and depreciation is available, budget planners do not need a formal capital budget to pursue an appropriate combination of government investment programs and overall budget surpluses (or deficits).

In the real world, of course, matters are different. Even after six years of budget deficits between $150 and $220 billion, the concept of "budget balance" is still a potent political symbol in the United States. Historically, the power of the symbol did not stem principally from a reasoned view that budget deficits cause undesirable macroeconomic consequences. The source of its power is deeper than rational analysis, and seems to be peculiarly American. James Savage has persuasively argued that the roots of hostility to budget deficits go back to the Jeffersonian-Jacksonian-agrarian fear of excessive government, whose tendency to be "corrupted" through recourse to debt had to be suppressed.[18] Over the years balanced budgets also became associated with the idea of "prudent management" and "administrative efficiency."[19] Finally, wartime experience in the United States and other countries combined with warnings of conservative politicians and some economists have linked large budget deficits with inflation in the public minds.

In an economy of divided powers, with appropriations in the hands of a Congress under powerful parochial pressures to create or expand specific governmental programs, some "supra-rational" check on the ability of government to run a deficit may be needed. Arguments of some economists to the contrary notwithstanding, legislators, in the absence of a strong public aversion to budget deficits, find borrowing less onerous than raising taxes. To be sure, the appeal of a balanced budget has sometimes deterred desirable spending increases or tax cuts during recessions. On balance, however, the political symbol of a balanced budget is probably a useful check on a mild bias in the budget-making system toward deficits. It is one of many implicit constraints on majoritarian decisionmaking whose great

---

[18] James D. Savage, *Balanced Budgets and American Politics*, Cornell University Press (1988), esp. chapter 4. The term "corruption" was then used not to denote chicanery or fraud but an unwarranted expansion of government power.

[19] Thomas Anton, "Roles and Symbols in the Determination of State Expenditure," *Midwest Journal of Political Science*, February 1967 (cited in Savage, p. 5).

advantage over Constitutional constraints lies in their flexibility and the
fact they can occasionally, and usefully, be breached.[20]

The symbol has generally been effective, but—quite obviously—not
completely so. Up until the 1980s structural budget deficits in the United
States tended to be rather small (see Table 1). Apart from war and deep
recession, the structural deficits averaged about 1 percent of national
income. I consider the string of huge deficits of the 1980s to be a unique
event. The 1981 decisions that created them—a huge tax cut combined
with a massive defense buildup—were not adopted with the warning that
they would lead to large budget deficits. In its 1981 budget submission, the
incoming Reagan administration forecast a budget surplus of $30 billion by
1986 if its tax and expenditure policies were adopted. Even without the $30
billion of unidentified ("asterisk") budget cuts included in its budget message, the federal budget was then projected to come into balance by 1986.
Once the tax and defense programs had been adopted, and the underlying
economic assumptions proven wildly optimistic, rising interest payments
on the rapidly mounting Federal debt offset the many cuts in nondefense
civilian spending that were in fact made. Then a political impasse over the
wisdom of raising taxes kept the deficit high.

In sum, the goal of a balanced budget has been and remains a useful, if
imperfect and occasionally counterproductive, discipline on the Federal
budget process, even if it has not been strong enough in the 1980s to
generate the political support needed to eliminate a large budget deficit
once that deficit has been created.

The moral of all of this is that budget accounting should recognize the
fact that the symbol of a balanced budget is a moderately potent and
generally benign political force. Consequently, one criterion in defining the
bottom line is to specify what should be included and excluded such that
we would generally be satisfied with a "balanced budget" in periods of
reasonably high employment. This criterion points to the exclusion of the
Social Security funds from the budget unless a large Social Security surplus, defined to be outside the budget, generated successful political pressure to liberalize benefits, an event I consider unlikely. Translation of the
surplus in those funds into increased national saving is more likely if we aim
for budget balance excluding Social Security than if we include Social
Security in the budget and aim, by the mid-1990s, for an overall surplus
equal to the annual trust fund accumulation.

If I am right about the continuing political force and normative useful-

---

[20] They are analogous to implicit contracts in labor market theory which help make
possible productivity-enhancing long-term relationships between employer and employee without the potentially stultifying rigidity of long-term written contracts.

ness of the balanced budget symbol, several other implications follow: First, the political attraction of the balanced budget symbol can be harmful if it tends to interfere with running the automatic deficits that occur in recessions. The markedly greater stability of the post-World War II economy, in contrast to the economic volatility of the late nineteenth and early twentieth centuries, has been attributed by many studies importantly to the automatic stabilizing effects of the postwar federal budget system.[21] Thus, the budget deficit, on which the media focuses, ought ideally to be a standardized high-employment budget. The obstacle to using this standard is, I think, a fear that somehow the White House and the Office of Management and Budget might sometimes manipulate such a standard to understate the size of the deficit. A new budget reform law, therefore, should mandate one or two key parameters to be used in standardizing the deficit. For purposes of matching the publicly reported deficit to the deficit appropriate for internal budgetary planning, it is essential that the *changes* in the measure of the deficit used for evaluating policy arise from changes in tax or expenditures policy, and not from changes in the cyclical position of the economy.

Recognizing the political potency of the balanced budget symbol acknowledges the political content of accounting definitions. Adoption of a capital budget for the Federal Government would almost surely expose decisions to classify outlays as "current" or "capital" transactions to strong political pressures. If "capital" expenditures do not count against achievement of a balanced budget, classification will obviously become an important element of political bargaining. It is no coincidence that support for capital budgets usually comes either from those who favor outlays that have a good chance of being classified as capital or from those who generally favor higher government outlays and want to minimize the reported size of deficits. In any event, given current outlays, adoption of a capital budget for the Federal Government would not relax pressures to cut the deficit. A capital budget not only permits exclusion of capital outlays from the budget, but also requires adding back an allowance for depreciation to the operating budget. Federal capital outlays, outside defense, have been so modest in recent years that a capital budget would only lower the currently reported federal deficit by $8 billion.[22] Treating federal education outlays as

---

[21] J. Bradford DeLong and Lawrence H. Summers, "The Changing Cyclical Variability of Economic Activity in the U.S.," *NBER Working Paper #1450*, Sept. 1984; C. Schultze, *Other Times, Other Places*, Brookings (1986), Lecture II, pp. 59-79.

[22] $8 billion is the value, expressed in current prices, of the 1987 increase in the net stock of nonmilitary federal capital assets, as reported by the Department of Commerce, in its estimates of tangible reproducible wealth (*Survey of Current Business*, August 1988, p. 87).

capital hardly changes the calculation. If current federal expenditures on education are classified as capital outlays, depreciation would have to be added to the operating budget for the loss of value on past outlays. If the federally financed "stock" of educational capital is depreciated at the very conservative rate of 3 percent a year, the net reduction in the budget deficit also amounts only to about $8 billion.[23]

While the balanced budget symbol is still a useful political force, it was not a completely effective one even before 1980. As noted earlier, structural deficits in nonwar, nonrecession years before 1980 averaged 1 percent of NNP. And so in the prior section I argued that to achieve the "target" national saving rate—which would be consistent with a budget deficit (excluding Social Security) in the neighborhood of 1 percent of GNP—one ought to plan and aim for budget balance. Of course, once it was agreed that a "small" deficit was acceptable, that deficit amount would then become the target from which further slippage would occur. Since the target saving rate probably errs on the side of being too low anyway, a flat old-fashioned zero target for the long-run budget deficit ought to be enforced as closely as possible.

Is it likely that taking the Social Security (and other retirement) trust funds "off-budget" could also have unintentional political consequences? In the 1960s and early 1970s, the projection of Social Security revenues was based on the then unrealistic assumption of constant real wages. When tax rates were set to "balance" the fund over 75 years, subsequent increases in real wages led to projected surpluses that, it is widely believed, generated political pressure for raising benefits.[24] With the Social Security surpluses included in the Gramm-Rudman-Hollings targets, the pressures for containing expenditures that are exerted by a huge consolidated budget deficit swamp any pressures to liberalize benefits growing out of the existence of large surpluses in the fund. But what would happen if, in public perceptions as well as official accounting, reductions in the Social Security surplus no longer added to "the" budget deficit? Would this situation set up incentives for benefit liberalization? I think the danger in the 1990s will be far less than it was in the 1960s. Among the educated and interested public, and among legislators, wide consensus has been reached that the current working generation ought to help "pay for its own retirement," and that the

---

[23] These are very rough estimates based on an accumulation of historical educational outlays by the Federal government, applying the 3 percent depreciation rate to get a net stock.

[24] See the discussion in Martha Derthick, *Policymaking for Social Security*, Brookings (1979), pp. 348-51, and C. Schultze, "Budget Alternatives After Vietnam," in *Agenda for the Nation*, Kermit Gordon, ed., Brookings (1968), pp. 27, 42.

Social Security trust funds ought to be kept in actuarial balance at least over the next 75 years. These two conditions in combination imply the accumulation of sizable reserves. They also imply that benefit liberalization must be matched by immediate tax increases. I believe that the political force of the implicit contract to maintain the sanctity of trust fund financing will dominate the tendency to spend reserves. However, it would be wise if major political leaders periodically reasserted the importance of the implicit contract, to prevent past history from repeating itself.

While the Social Security and Medicare trust funds should be removed from the conventional budget, no further steps should be taken to privatize the two programs. The "redistributive" and the "insurance" objectives of the Social Security program have always been partly in conflict.[25] Basing the program on earmarked taxes and relating the benefits to prior wages, even if not proportionally, promotes the idea that the program represents an inviolable insurance contract. Making the benefits schedule progressive moves the program in the direction of "welfare."

Various suggestions have been made that would move the system toward the pure insurance concept: Removing the program from the Department of Health and Human Services and placing it under the direction of a bipartisan council or commission, and investing the assets in private as well as government securities, are two such suggestions. A newly published study of Social Security financing by Aaron, Bosworth, and Burtless[26] argues that investing the Social Security surpluses in private instead of Federal Government securities would make little difference to financial markets, and—adjusted for risk—would not raise overall economic growth. But both of these ideas, if adopted, would make Social Security appear more like a private "businesslike" insurance system. In turn, over a long span of years, that attitude could lead to a weakening of broad public support for the redistributive elements of the program and possibly give rise to various schemes to privatize part or all of the system. Those who find the current mix of the two elements in the system about right should oppose such changes.[27] And so, apart from altering the budgetary classifica-

---

[25] See, for example, W. Andrew Achenbaum, *Social Security, Visions and Revisions,* Cambridge University Press (1986), Chapter 1; and Martha Derthick, *Policymaking for Social Security,* Brookings (1979), esp. Chapter 10.

[26] Henry J. Aaron, Barry B. Bosworth, and Gary Burtless, *Can America Afford to Grow Old? Paying for Social Security and Medicare,* Brookings, 1988.

[27] If Social Security benefits were taxed more like the income from private contributory pension funds, which would require taxation of about 85 rather than the current 50 percent of benefits, and the proceeds placed in the *general* fund, the fairness of the system as a whole would be improved.

tion of the funds, I would not favor organizational or financial changes along the lines suggested above.

Some have proposed that part of Social Security reserves be earmarked to finance federal capital projects, perhaps through special federal "investment project" bonds that would keep such outlays off-budget. The operating budget would pay only the interest and amortization on such obligations. While additional federal investment in infrastructures is desirable, taking such outlays off-budget would generate continuing political infighting and politically inspired decisions about what ought and ought not to be labelled "capital." Programs so defined as capital outlays would be favored over those that were not. On balance, this suggestion is a bad idea.

Finally, although the budget target should be set to yield a balance outside the Social Security funds, it would not be politically productive to incorporate that target into budget plans over the next four years. Reaching a balanced budget with the Social Security surpluses included will be difficult enough. Proposing now the additional phased tax increases and expenditure cuts sufficient to achieve a large surplus in the combined budget might well strike the public and the Congress as such a large task as to perpetuate stalemate. Hence, achieving the desired objective of national saving should be seen as a two-stage process: balancing the budget *including* Social Security by 1993 and balancing the budget *excluding* Social Security by 1998.

DISCUSSION

Lawrence H. Thompson*

C HARLES SCHULTZE HAS DONE AN EXCELLENT JOB OF answering three questions: He argues that a good case can be made for a higher national saving rate. He holds that government budget policy provides an appropriate and effective mechanism for achieving a higher saving rate. And he judges that the projected Social Security buildup comes close to his assessment of how much highe⁻ the saving rate should be.

I have no important criticisms of his analysis and no keen insights about additional issues that should have been considered. His paper is clear, concise, and persuasive. It allows us to conclude that a sensible medium-term goal would be the achievement of a surplus in the total budget of roughly the size of the surplus currently projected for Social Security.

That goal will not be reached in the next year or two; it may take anywhere from five to ten years to get there. During that time, Schultze and others will have ample opportunity to fine-tune this analysis and decide whether the targets should be raised or lowered. For the time being, making steady progress toward Schultze's goal is sufficiently ambitious.

While I agree with the paper's basic message, others may not. Some will disagree with his economic analysis, others will doubt that the political process will produce the result he desires.

Disagreements arise, in part, because the current debate over Social Security financing contains two strands that intersect over the implications of accumulating large Social Security reserves. One debate views the current Social Security financing from the perspective of traditional Social Security program considerations. The other views it from the perspective of recent trends and possible desirable future paths in aggregate U.S. saving.

Both debates focus on the implications of flows into and out of the Social Security trust funds, which are special accounts at the U.S. Treasury.

---

* Assistant Comptroller General, General Accounting Office.

Because the Social Security program has not been allowed to overdraw its Treasury account, projections of future trust fund flows are prepared regularly in order to see whether scheduled revenues will suffice to cover scheduled benefits. Traditionally, Congress uses these projections in deciding whether to change payroll tax rates or pension benefits.

The Treasury, as Social Security banker, receives a net cash inflow when Social Security runs a surplus and experiences a net cash outflow when it runs a deficit. If not offset by a deficit in other Treasury operations, Social Security surpluses produce a positive overall net cash flow for the Federal government, allow the Treasury to reduce the value of Federal debt in the hands of the public, and increase national saving.

Those primarily interested in the effects of the Social Security financing debate on the Social Security program focus on the time path of the balance in the trust fund account and pay little or no attention to implications for national saving. They are concerned about possible political effects of the current financing pattern. For example, some believe Congress is more likely to increase benefits if the trust fund balance is large than if it is small. If they consider such liberalizations undesirable, they may oppose the current Social Security financing plan. Note, however, that their reasons involve program considerations and have nothing to do with macroeconomics.

Others who fear benefit cuts when annual Social Security revenues are projected to be less than annual outlays may favor accumulation of the reserves, in the hope that large reserves will reduce the likelihood of such cuts. Again, this is a reason that has nothing to do with macroeconomics.

The second debate concerns possible government actions to deal with the recent collapse in the national saving rate. In the context of this debate, many favor a modest Federal budget surplus that would add to the pool of private saving rather than the sizable recent deficits that have served as a substantial drain on saving. Note that it is an overall budget surplus that counts, not whether the surplus is in the Social Security program or elsewhere.

These two debates merge in large measure because of the demographic shift that will occur when the baby boom generation retires. At that time, the Social Security benefits currently legislated will consume a significantly higher fraction of our national income than they do currently. But a higher national saving rate today could help to offset the increase in future Social Security costs, leaving tomorrow's workers no worse off (that is, with after-tax incomes not lower) than if the demographic shift had not occurred. In other words, we can "advance fund" the burden of the demographic shift by assuring that the scheduled Social Security surpluses translate into increased capital formation.

I am as guilty as anyone of making this linkage. Early in 1986 a GAO report noted that if the Social Security surpluses could be translated into an increase of only 0.1 percentage point in the annual rate of increase in real wages, the faster productivity growth would quickly offset the higher payroll tax burden.[1] And, in a paper I co-authored with Henry Aaron later in 1986, we used a simple model that Ned Gramlich had developed to show that the surpluses now projected might be sufficient to offset the higher Social Security burden provided they are translated into increased investment.[2] More recently, Aaron, Burtless, and Bosworth, and Anderson and his co-authors have shown that increases in savings of roughly the magnitude that the projected surpluses can produce are sufficient to compensate future workers for the higher Social Security costs.[3]

Having confessed sympathy with this line of reasoning, let me now point out its weaknesses. First, under current projections, the increase in the retiree-to-worker ratio that occurs when the baby boom generation retires is not temporary; the higher ratios continue after the baby boom generation has passed through the system. Yet, under current law, the balance in the Social Security account first rises and then falls so that any contributions to increased capital formation will be only temporary if current law remains in effect. If capital formation produced by Social Security surpluses is to offset the permanently increased burden of Social Security benefits, either the balance in the fund must not be drawn down or the effect of that draw-down on capital formation must somehow be offset.

Second, although higher savings today can compensate future workers for higher future Social Security burdens, the future workers will probably never recognize that they have been compensated. Suppose that a far-sighted nineteenth century Congress recognized that citizens of the twentieth century would have to bear increased burdens to finance national

---

[1] *Social Security: Past Projections and Future Financing Concerns* GAO/HRD-86-22, March 11, 1986).

[2] Henry J. Aaron and Lawrence H. Thompson, "Social Security and the Economists," prepared for the Conference on Social Security After Fifty, George Washington University, March 19, 1986.

[3] H. Aaron, B. Bosworth, and G. Burtless, *Final Report to Social Security Administration, U.S. Department of Health and Human Services, on Contract No. 600-87-0072 to the Brookings Institution,* 1988; and J. Anderson, R. Kuzmack, D. Morgan, G. Schink, D. Jorgenson, and R.M. Perrandin, "Study of the Potential Economic and Fiscal Effects of Investment of the Assets of the Old Age and Survivors' Insurance and Disability Insurance Trust Funds." Final Report Submitted to U.S. Department of Health and Human Services, Social Security Administration, May 1988. See also H. Aaron, B. Bosworth, and G. Burtless, *Can America Afford to Grow Old? Paying for Social Security,* The Brookings Institution, Washington, D.C., 1989.

defense and decided to promote capital formation — say by awarding land grants to encourage the building of railroads. Such an action might have accelerated the growth of national income enough to offset the higher defense burden. Even if such a scenario could be demonstrated, would it change our attitudes today about the fraction of our national income we want to devote to defense spending? I doubt it. Similarly, even if Social Security surpluses add to national saving, I doubt it will change significantly the attitude of future workers toward the higher burden of financing Social Security. If I am correct, this form of "advance funding" of the Social Security burden is an analytical exercise with essentially no political meaning.

Because the higher Social Security burden will be permanent, not temporary, and because future workers are unlikely to realize that they have been compensated for the higher Social Security burden, this debate over Social Security financing really concerns whether the saving rate should be increased for reasons unconnected with Social Security. Although I agree in general with the position advanced by Schultze, those of us who share this view need to recognize that it rests on several frequently tacit assumptions. The argument is strengthened to the extent that: a) we rest the case for increasing national saving on factors other than the retirement costs of the baby boom generation; b) we are fairly sure that the accumulation of large reserves will not encourage undesirable future program changes; and c) we recognize that any near-term increase in saving should not be eroded by a future drop in the saving rate. We also must recognize that persons who agree with the Schultze economic analysis may nevertheless disagree with his policy prescription either because they fear induced benefit increases or because they believe that what is needed is a permanent increase in saving rather than the possible temporary additions to saving through accumulation of Social Security reserves.

DISCUSSION

Rudolph G. Penner*

I T IS NEVER A PLEASURE TO DISCUSS ONE OF CHARLES
Schultze's papers. They are too darn good. They leave you little to say.
Having been frustrated in trying to find any flaws in Schultze's
economics, I shall begin with the end of the paper where he becomes a
political scientist. I find political truths harder to identify than economic
ones, but that makes it easier for a discussant because almost anything can
be alleged without fear that it can be proved logically wrong. Logic plays
little role in politics.

I share Schultze's concern over the low national saving rate and agree
that the most straightforward way of increasing national saving is to lower
the overall Federal budget deficit. I worry little that increased public saving
will lower private saving, and I probably worry even less than Schultze that
the contractionary impact of deficit reduction will create problems for the
economy that cannot be corrected by monetary policy.

The key political question then becomes whether some change in the
budget process would ease the task of deficit reduction. I will focus only on
one, a change in the single deficit measure that is targeted. Schultze would
put the OASDI, HI and civil service retirement trust funds truly off budget
and enunciate long-run targets for the deficit that remains.

I fear that this proposition and my discussion of it will seem absurd to
those who have not been intimately involved in budget struggles. In the
abstract, it should not be that difficult to have more than one target—one
for the overall deficit and others that reflect trade-offs among non-trust
fund and trust fund accounts. But budgeting is extraordinarily complex,
with tens of thousands of decisions having to be made in a relatively short
time. It is necessary to economize on the need for information and this is
frequently done using crude rules of thumb. There is, in other words, a

---

*Senior Fellow, The Urban Institute.

rational need for irrational procedures. The trick is to find rules of thumb that ease the task without doing too much damage to the efficiency of the result. Having one deficit target rather than many is important to achieve this end.

Schultze believes that by focusing on the non-trust fund deficit, the seriousness of the deficit problem will become more apparent and more vigorous actions to reduce the deficit will follow. He relies on the power of a set of myths to instill budget discipline—the myth that a balanced budget is always good, which he hopes will encourage responsibility in the non-trust fund accounts, and the myth that some sort of actuarial balance should be maintained in the trust funds. The myths have frayed in recent years as the budget has been far from balanced and the OASDI and HI trust funds together are far from actuarial balance. But he apparently believes that the myths retain sufficient power to produce decisions leading to a smaller deficit if his recommendation is adopted than would result if it is not.

I am skeptical. In particular, I worry that if the trust funds totally escape the budget and if benefit increases do not count against "the official budget deficit," the loss of control over the trust funds will cost more than the savings that can be achieved in the non-trust fund accounts. Even if this is not true, the incentive to find savings in the trust funds will be greatly diminished. Savings in Medicare and civil service pensions have been significant in recent years. I doubt that they would have been as significant if, in making cuts, the Congress had not obtained credit for reducing "the deficit." More savings are crucial in the future, particularly in Medicare.

More fundamentally, I strongly believe that trust fund expenditures should be traded off against other expenditures in the budget process. I agree that trust funds are governed by a moral contract, but moral contracts, like legal contracts, should be subject to renegotiation as conditions change. And conditions have changed greatly in recent years. Life expectancy at age 65 has soared; the cost of medical care has risen even more; and economic growth has slowed.

Beyond all of these considerations, the Congress should be vitally concerned with how much the Federal government will be drawing from private capital markets every year, and the unified budget deficit is a good, if not perfect, measure of that. It should also be concerned with the government's draw on national saving every year, and although the unified budget deficit is not a very accurate measure of that—the National Income Accounts deficit is better—it is close enough for government work. For all of these reasons, I would reject Schultze's proposed approach to targeting and prefer to continue to target the unified or overall deficit.

I have few complaints about his masterful discussion of the economics of saving and growth. I might, however, have given more emphasis to a couple of points.

First, if national saving rises, it is crucial to know whether the added saving increases domestic capital formation or reduces capital inflows from abroad. The latter provides a much lower social rate of return because we lose the tax revenues on foreign-owned equity. It also fails to increase the productivity and wages of domestic workers, but it does raise the rate of return to domestic capital and it saves us from having to transfer as much income abroad.

Second and more controversially, Schultze's analysis proceeds as though the rate of capital formation and the rate of technological progress were completely independent. I have never been persuaded by Ed Denison's argument that they are independent, and I prefer to believe that capital investment is essential to implement a considerable portion of technological change. This would have the effect of raising the social rate of return to increased saving, and suggests that considerable attention should be paid to gross saving and investment as well as to net saving and investment. The recent path of gross saving is not as disturbing as that of net saving, but it must be emphasized that it is not so good as to rationalize the huge budget deficits that have been experienced in recent years.

Neither of these economic quibbles is important enough to alter the basic economic conclusions or philosophy of the paper. It is only the politics that bothers me.

COSTS OF THE AGING POPULATION: IMPLICATIONS FOR CURRENT BUDGET POLICY

REAL AND IMAGINED BURDENS OF AN AGING AMERICA

Henry J. Aaron*

T WO DECADES REMAIN BEFORE THE RETIREMENT OF the baby boom generation begins. The increase in costs associated with that event is not temporary but permanent. The proportion of the population that is elderly will not fall again unless birth rates or immigration rise sharply or mortality rates increase.

In anticipation of this event, a prudent nation, one might think, would be trying to boost saving and add to productive capacity, so that the increased costs of benefits for the expanded ranks of beneficiaries could be met without unduly burdening future workers. The Japanese, for example, often point to demographic trends similar to those the United States will be confronting when asked to explain why they save so much.

Rather than boosting saving, however, the United States has been doing just the opposite by pursuing an overall budget policy of breathtaking prodigality. The national saving rate, now barely 3 percent of net national product, is well below half the average rate since World War II. The foreign trade deficits are still appalling by any standard other than our own dismal record of the past few years. By reducing saving and depleting foreign

*Senior Fellow, The Brookings Institution. This paper is based upon the recent book by Aaron, Barry T. Bosworth, and Gary Burtless, *Can America Afford to Grow Old? Paying for Social Security,* The Brookings Institution, 1988.

assets, you and I can consume more than if we limited ourselves to what we are producing. In so doing, however, we bequeath to our children a smaller domestic capital stock than we could have given them if we had saved more at home and borrowed less abroad. And we shall leave them with more foreign debt than assets, in sharp contrast to the large excess of assets over debt that the United States had less than a decade ago.

This introduction may sound more appropriate for a conference on budget or trade policy than it does for a session on the costs of an aging population. But as the title of this session makes clear, the future burdens of support for the elderly are closely related to current budget policy. In the course of my remarks, I shall try to explain why. I shall also try to dispel some widespread misunderstandings about the way the elderly may or may not place economic burdens on the rest of the population.

Burdens—Real and Imagined

Everyone here has been subjected to what might be called "the horrible ratios." The number of workers per retiree, you are told, was once very high—more than ten to one in 1950. It is much lower today—barely three to one. And, you are portentously warned, it will sink as low as two to one in coming decades. This trend evokes the image of a shrinking population of toiling workers forced to work ever longer to produce goods for a swelling mass of idle elderly. Following the recitation of these ratios often comes a warning that we have promised more to the elderly than our children will be able to deliver, that we must cut benefits, and the sooner the better.

There is only one thing wrong with citing these ratios. *They tell exactly nothing about whether the growing numbers of retirees will or will not impose burdens on tomorrow's workers.* Even worse, they divert attention from the indicators that do show whether and how large those burdens will be.

To demonstrate why the ratio of workers to retirees is worse than useless as a measure of the burdens the elderly will impose on others, I ask you to consider what economic burden I will impose on others if in the course of my lifetime I consume no more than my earnings plus the income on any saving that I may have done. Having consumed only what I earned or accumulated through saving, I will have used no more than I have contributed to the economy through my labor and saving. In short, I impose no economic burden on others.

This line of reasoning applies whether I choose to retire early or late in my life. To be sure, I may impose emotional burdens on my spouse, my children, or others, and I might impose burdens on others if I do not pay enough in taxes to cover the costs of public services that I enjoy. But if I do not receive more in public services than I have paid in taxes, and if my private accounts are balanced in the sense I have just described, I will have paid my economic way.

This line of reasoning applies not just to me as an individual, but to all members of each age cohort in the population. It means that the mere fact that a larger or smaller proportion of the population is elderly tells nothing about the burdens that each cohort imposes on others. Whether each cohort imposes burdens on younger age groups does not depend on its size relative to the rest of the population, but rather on whether or not it has paid its dues, in the sense that it produces during its life as much as it consumes.[1]

In short, the size of the baby boom cohorts and of others that will follow them has nothing to do with whether they become a burden on future workers. Rather, each cohort will impose no burden if it consumes no more than it produces. It will impose a burden if it consumes more. The critical question, therefore, is whether the baby boom generation is paying its way.

The "Baby Boomer" Balance Sheet

I am going to focus on three of the many economic transactions each age cohort has with the rest of the population: Social Security pension benefits; publicly financed health benefits; and the rest of the budget.[2] Is the baby boom generation likely to pay as much in taxes as it collects in benefits?

---

[1] Economists will recognize that the process by which each cohort pays its own way is simply an expression of the life-cycle theory of consumption behavior. If all cohorts behave in this fashion, the capital stock will grow at a rate equal to the sum of the rates of growth of income per worker and of population. Whether the resulting capital stock is too high or too low to enable successive cohorts to consume as much as possible over their lifetimes depends on whether the rate of return to saving is greater or less than this sum of growth rates. If the interest rate is higher (lower), then welfare would be increased (decreased) by a rise in saving. In this model, no individual leaves any unconsumed income at death to add to saving. Nevertheless, each cohort adds to the capital stock because part of its income is unconsumed throughout its life; and the sum of these unconsumed quantities grows as the population rises and output per worker increases. Clearly, if each cohort leaves significant net bequests to the next, as recent work by Laurence Kotlikoff and Lawrence Summers suggests, the argument is strengthened. See Laurence T. Kotlikoff and Lawrence H. Summers, "The Role of Intergenerational Transfers in Aggregate Capital Accumulation," *Journal of Political Economy*, vol. 89 (August 1981), pp. 706–732. Also see Franco Modigliani, "The Role of Intergenerational Transfers and Life Cycle Saving in the Accumulation of Wealth," *The Journal of Economic Perspectives*, vol. 2, (Spring 1988) pp. 15–40 and Laurence J. Kotlikoff, "Intergenerational Transfers and Savings," *The Journal of Economic Perspectives*, vol. 2, (spring 1988) pp. 41–58.

[2] In addition, of course, each cohort receives sustenance from its parents and cares for its own children. While such private transfers are worthy of attention in totaling up the accounts for each cohort, I shall ignore them here. For an informal discussion of these transfers, see Henry J. Aaron, "Silver Threads: Pension and Health Policy for an Aging Society," paper presented at the Williams College Series on Social Policy, November 29, 1988.

Social Security

Each cohort pays payroll taxes through its working life and receives retirement, survivors, and disability benefits under stipulated conditions. A cohort imposes no burdens on others if the present value of the payroll taxes it pays is as great as the present value of the benefits paid on its behalf. It imposes a burden if the value of benefits exceeds the value of taxes paid.

Several studies indicate that the baby boom cohorts, defined as those who will reach age 65 in the quarter century following the year 2010, will receive back in benefits just about what they paid in taxes. On the average, given current economic and demographic assumptions, the value of benefits will return to each cohort the taxes they have paid plus a rate of interest, in addition to full compensation for inflation, of about 2 percent per year.[3] Some members of each cohort—recipients of low wages and large families, for example—will do better. Some members of each cohort—highly paid wage-earners and those who were single all of their lives, for example—will do worse. But each cohort will get back about what it paid in taxes, fully adjusted for inflation, plus a real rate of return about equal to the rate economists have long estimated to be the safe rate of return earned over the last several decades.[4]

The same point can be seen another way. At present, Social Security absorbs about 5.4 percent of net national product. When the baby boom generation is fully retired, Social Security benefits will be a bit over 7 percent of net national product, an increase of about 1.8 percent of net national product. Under current law, the Social Security trust funds are projected to accumulate large reserves, rising to about 30 percent of net national product. If fiscal policy is managed so that these reserves add to national saving, the increase in national output will more than offset these added Social Security costs. Whether through good planning or dumb luck, Congress has set a tax schedule for Old-Age, Survivors, and Disability Insurance that effectively relieves future workers of any of the burden they would otherwise bear from the increase in the number of retirees.[5]

---

[3] Robert J. Myers and Bruce D. Schobel, "A Money's-Worth Analysis of Social Security Retirement Benefits," *Transactions*, Society of Actuaries, 1983, pp. 533–561.

[4] The Myers-Schobel estimates are based on the Social Security rules as amended in 1983. With the passage of time, it is likely that current methods of computing long-term actuarial balance will require Congress either to raise payroll taxes or cut benefits to maintain long-term balance. The exact timing of such adjustments is impossible to forecast, but it could affect some members of the baby boom generation. In that event, the implied rate of return would be reduced.

[5] For a full examination of the effects of alternative methods of paying for Social Security on the course of economic growth, see Aaron, Bosworth, and Burtless, 1988.

In short, the baby boom generation is not going to impose burdens on future workers through Social Security, because today's workers are paying a fair price for the benefits they will receive. Consequently, no basis exists for cutting Social Security benefits on the grounds that they will be excessively burdensome in the future. To be sure, the nation should periodically reexamine the role the elderly should play in the economy and the proper scope of Social Security, including what proportions of income retirees should receive from social insurance, private pensions, private saving, and means-tested or income-tested benefits. But this debate should not be shadowed by the fiction that Social Security benefits promised under current law will place undue burdens on future workers.

Health Benefits

While today's workers are paying in full for the pension benefits they will be receiving, the same cannot be said for health benefits. Where the Social Security system is scheduled to accumulate large reserves, the payroll taxes allocated to Medicare Hospital Insurance are just about sufficient to cover costs for today's beneficiaries. The number of current beneficiaries is smaller and the per capita cost of hospitalization is lower than they will be in the future. Furthermore, three-quarters of the cost of physicians' services reimbursed under part B of Medicare comes from the general budget, a point that I will turn to more later.

Thus, if one confines one's attention to Medicare, today's workers will impose sizable burdens on future workers. Estimates we have made at Brookings suggest that the increased future costs of Medicare hospital benefits will rise to a maximum of about 2 percent of net national product. Such estimates are shadowed by all of the uncertainty surrounding the progress of medical technology and the rate of economic growth, but they indicate the general size of the additional costs. Although we have not estimated the analogous costs for physicians' benefits, they are of the same order of magnitude.

These calculations ignore future increases in the cost of long-term care. Long-term care services are consumed primarily by people over age 75—a group that will increase from about 5 percent of the population today to nearly 12 percent by 2040—and especially by those over age 85, who will comprise nearly 5 percent of the U.S. population by the middle of the next century, four times the current proportion. However these benefits are financed, the resources used to provide them will come from future production. If steps are not taken now to add to national saving in anticipation of these costs, long-term care for the baby boom generation will impose costs on future workers.

Table 1
Federal Budget Deficit With and Without Retirement
Trust Funds, Fiscal Years 1988–1994

	1988	1989	1994	Change: 1988–1994
Total Federal Deficit	− 155	− 155	− 122	+ 33
Less Surplus in:				
Social Security (OASDI) (off-budget)	39	56	117	+ 78
On Budget Deficit (Unified)	− 194	− 211	− 239	− 45
Less Surplus in:				
Medicare (HI)	16	20	12	− 4
Fed. Employ. Retirement	34	35	48	+ 14
General Fund Nonretirement Deficit	− 244	− 266	− 299	− 55

Source: Congressional Budget Office, *The Economic and Budget Outlook—Fiscal Years 1990–1994* (January 1989) and unpublished tables.

And there is more: many private employers now promise health benefits to retirees but have not set aside reserves adequate to meet these obligations. The present value of such benefits is estimated to be between $169 billion and $275 billion.[6] Meeting these costs will require diversion of future production. The lack of reserves means that current saving has not been increased to enhance future productive capacity to help meet those costs.

The Rest of the Budget

Fiscal policy and retirement policy are ordinarily regarded as separate subjects. To paraphrase the immortal words of a former president, it would be easy to make such a distinction, but it would be wrong.

The current debate about the financing of Social Security and Medicare illustrates the inextricable link between the financing of ordinary govern-

---

[6] The lower estimate was prepared by the Employee Benefit Research Institute (EBRI); the higher, by the Government Accounting Office. I reduced the GAO estimate by roughly 32 percent, EBRI's estimate of the reduction in costs attributable to the 1988 catastrophic health care cost amendments to the Medicare system. Each estimate includes benefits for current retirees, accrued benefits of active workers, and future accruals of active workers. The difference is traceable to estimates of the numbers of workers who will retire with entitlements to such benefits and to differences in the assumed rates of growth of health care costs.

ment services and retirement policy as expressed in the financing of retirement benefits. Table 1 reports the the Congressional Budget Office's early-1989 projections of the Federal Government deficit under current policy. The overall deficit is projected to decline between 1988 and 1994, because of a growing surplus in retirement programs and despite an increasing deficit in the rest of government operations.

The economic justification for additions to Social Security reserves is that such surpluses increase national saving, add to the U.S. capital stock, and boost productive capacity in anticipation of the extra costs a growing population of retirees will generate. Current budget policy overwhelms this sound policy. Instead of adding to U.S. national saving, current fiscal policy simply diverts a part of payroll taxes to pay for ordinary operations of government. To put matters another way, although the baby boom generation is and will be paying fully for the Social Security benefits it will eventually receive, it is picking the pockets of future workers by failing to pay for current government consumption. In short, the Social Security pension system is not a device by which current workers are saddling future workers with any burden at all. But general budget policy and the inadequate financing of health benefits are doing exactly that—imposing avoidable burdens on the future.

What Should Be Done?

In preparing for an aging population, the United States must decide whether the benefits it is providing are reasonable and, given benefit commitments, whether financing is adequate.

Social Security

On this score, I suggest that Social Security policy rates very high marks. Although Social Security benefits remain modest—averaging only $521 per month for new retiree awards, $475 for new disability awards, and $342 for new awards for widows and widowers in June 1988—they have been a major element in the climb of the elderly into approximate economic parity with the rest of the U.S. population.[7] The decision in 1972 to adjust Social Security benefits automatically for inflation, although flawed in execution and later amended, assures beneficiaries incomes that are invariant with respect to inflation. Current financing, based on calculations stretching seventy-five years into the future and calling for the accumulation of large reserves, is highly conservative. Although some of the assumptions used in making these projections are probably too optimistic, others are unduly

---

[7] See Henry J. Aaron, *Economic Effects of Social Security,* The Brookings Institution, 1982.

pessimistic; on balance, the projections are reasonable, and the size of reserve accumulation assures Congress ample time to modify these assumptions in light of new information.[8] The financing of retirement, survivors, and disability insurance holds the potential, through increased capital formation, of adding to national output more than the additional costs that will be generated by the increased number of beneficiaries.

Room for debate about the structure of Social Security benefits remains. In particular, the failure to apply the same tax rules to Social Security benefits that are applied to private pensions remains an anomaly of the tax system. Extending to Social Security the rules now applied to private pensions could reduce the projected federal deficit by as much as $20 billion in 1993.

The proposals to adjust benefits for only part of increases in the cost of living, in contrast, make almost no sense whatsoever, as some simple examples illustrate. The proposals to limit cost-of-living increases to 60 percent of the rise in the consumer price index, as suggested by Peter Peterson, or to increase benefits 2 percent less than the rise in prices, as suggested for example by former Presidents Carter and Ford, amount to assuring the elderly and disabled steadily diminishing benefits the longer they remain on the benefit rolls. The two proposals, which are equivalent if the inflation rate is 5 percent, would mean that a 25-year-old disabled worker would find his benefit reduced by one-third by the time he or she reaches age 45 and by half by age 60. A 90 year old who retired at age 62 would find his or her benefit worth only 57 percent as much as it was on retirement.[9] The most charitable thing one can say of those who advance such proposals is that they have not thought through the implications of the proposal.

The striking characteristic of Old-Age, Survivors, and Disability Insurance is that it is working rather well. The elderly have achieved rough economic parity with the rest of the population. Social Security is the principal source of income for most of the elderly. Surveys document that the elderly complain no more or less than the non-elderly about most of the problems of daily living—income, housing, food, attention from relatives, and friendships—although most nonelderly persons think the elderly are beset with problems and the elderly too seem to think that other elderly

---

[8] For an examination of these assumptions, see Aaron, Bosworth, and Burtless, 1988, chapter 3.

[9] The rationale for the Peterson proposal is particularly hard to comprehend when inflation exceeds 5 percent. If prices rose 10 percent per year, for example, real benefits would be cut 4 percent per year. The purchasing power of the benefit of the 25-year-old disabled worker would be slashed 76 percent by the time he reached age 60.

persons are sorely afflicted.[10] Confronted with this evidence, we should not assume we are missing something but recognize that in this area government and private institutions both work reasonably well.

Health Care

The same cannot be said for public and private health care systems, which are suffering from numerous and diverse problems—rising costs, large numbers of uninsured, and uncovered services. While each of these topics is important, I focus here only on what would need to be done to make sure that the costs of any benefits we decide to offer the elderly will not impose undue burdens on future workers.

First, Medicare would have to accumulate reserves of a magnitude similar to those projected for Social Security pensions. These reserves would result from the establishment of taxes sufficient to pay for promised benefits on a long-term basis. They would boost national saving, add to the capital stock available to future workers, and boost future incomes. Whether current payroll taxes should be increased or some other revenue source should be developed is an important issue. But the key point is that steps should be taken now to increase saving in anticipation of large predictable increases in costs.

Second, the nation should begin to develop policies to help households meet the costs of long-term care. This step is important primarily to relieve households of heavy burdens many are ill-equipped to shoulder. But it is also important to act soon because the costs will be large, whether we rely primarily on private insurance or public programs, and it is time to begin amassing the reserves that will help pay for them.

Third, private employers should be required to begin funding liabilities for health benefits for future retirees, much as the Employee Retirement Income Security Act requires them gradually to create reserves for currently unfunded pension commitments.

Each of these steps requires that currently active workers and their employers shoulder the full costs of the benefits they will receive in the future. I am not suggesting that health benefits are overly generous. On the contrary, important extensions are desirable, such as improved protection against the costs of long-term care and measures to end our shameful failure to assure health insurance to nearly one American in six. Nor am I

---

[10] *The Myth and Reality of Aging in America*, A study for The National Council on the Aging, Inc. Louis Harris and Associates, Inc., June 1977; *Aging in the Eighties: America in Transition*, A study for The National Council on the Aging, Inc., Louis Harris and Associates, Inc., 1981.

denying the desirability of seeking increased efficiencies through technology assessment, increased competition, reformed reimbursement, and other modifications in the current system. My point is simply that whatever we may decide to do about the overall health care system, we should save now by accumulating reserves to meet the predictable consequences of our current promises.

The Rest of Fiscal Policy

Whenever the Federal Government runs a deficit, it must borrow a portion of private savings that would otherwise be available for investment in the United States or abroad. Sometimes deficits are reasonable. Whatever arguments can be made for such deficits, however, they are independent of the case for accumulating reserves for benefits promised to workers today for delivery in the future. Targets for the deficit or surplus in Federal Government activities for other operations of government should be set independently of the accumulation of reserves for promised future benefits such as those provided through Social Security and Medicare.

In the context of the current budget debate, the deficit on which attention should focus is that on operations of government other than pensions and Medicare. Measured in this way, the deficit in 1988 was $244 billion, not the $155 billion commonly cited in official discussions of the deficit. And the deficit is projected to rise to $299 billion in 1994. Whether an attempt should be made to cut that deficit to zero or to some other number, or to aim for a surplus, is an important issue to debate. But debate should focus on the deficit associated with activities of government other than retirement programs, if the reserves we are accumulating to help future workers meet those obligations are to serve that purpose.

Budget Policy Is Retirement Policy

The messages of this paper are simple.

- First, the growing numbers of elderly may impose burdens on future workers, but none is necessary if we take proper steps today. These steps consist simply in assuring that each cohort consumes no more than it contributes to production through its earnings and savings.
- Second, current pension policy satisfies this condition. The baby boom generation will earn no more than a fair rate of return on the contributions it is making to both public and private pensions.
- Third, the baby boom generation will end up consuming far more health care, both acute and long-term, than it is being asked to pay for under

current policy. This deficit will place a considerable burden on future workers.

- Fourth, the failure to collect in taxes enough to pay for current government consumption and the resulting erosion of national saving is the most serious financial burden that current workers are placing on future workers.

- Finally, whether the baby boom generation does or does not impose burdens on future workers has nothing to do with the commonly cited statistics on the ratio of retirees to active workers. People who cite these statistics either do not understand the issues or are intentionally misleading their readers and listeners.

The irony of this story should be clear. The policies most clearly identified as retirement policies, those under which public and private pensions are paid to retirees, are in good order, financed so that the baby boom cohorts will pay their way and not burden future workers. Poor financial management of government activities not clearly recognized as retirement policies threatens to undo the prudent legislation governing private and public pensions.

So too, ironically, does the failure, belatedly recognized, of public and private policies to address the problems of children and young adults, especially blacks, Native Americans, and Hispanics. Functional illiteracy, low educational achievement, teen-age pregnancy, and high unemployment all testify to poorly functioning families and failing private and public institutions. Actions to assist these groups are of overriding importance not just to them but to us all. It would be a sad mistake, however, if we used our growing awareness of these problems to justify cuts in private and public programs that for the first time in American history have brought the elderly economic equality.

COSTS OF THE AGING POPULATION: IMPLICATIONS FOR CURRENT BUDGET POLICY

FINANCING THE FUTURE: IS SOCIAL SECURITY THE PROBLEM OR THE SOLUTION?

Phillip J. Longman*

THE AGING OF THE POPULATION PRESENTS OUR ECONOMY with a straightforward challenge. Particularly as the baby boom generation reaches old age, fewer workers will be available to support each retiree. Similarly, we should expect that fewer taxpayers will be available to support each aircraft carrier, to carry each dollar of interest on the national debt, or to meet whatever the ongoing needs and obligations of government are in the next century.

As the ranks of the elderly swell in the next century, those of children will diminish. But what we save in government expenditures by having fewer children will likely be consumed many times over by the extra cost of providing for the old—at least if current budgetary patterns hold. At all levels of government, we now spend about three times per senior citizen what we spend per child—including the cost of public education.

That the United States should be running huge trade and budget deficits in this of all decades underscores the dimensions of the challenge before us. Currently, virtually the entire baby boom generation—one-third of the U.S. population—is in its prime, productive years. Moreover, an unprecedented proportion of the women of this generation are working for wages and contributing taxes. Yet even with this powerful demographic advantage, the

---

* Staff writer, *Florida Trend*. Author of *Born to Pay: The New Politics of Aging*.

United States cannot, or at least does not, pay its bills. What will happen when this anomalously large generation reaches old age, and begins to consume far more than it produces?

The short answer is: we do not know. But as the baby boom generation retires from the workplace, it stands to reason that the American standard of living will fall, unless each remaining worker at the time is able and willing to produce enough extra goods and services to compensate for the extra cost of supporting a relatively large number of retirees. That condition may come about automatically, but we have no right to assume it will, particularly in light of the mounting poverty rates among today's children, the general mediocrity of our schools, and the enormous public debts we are charging to the future. Instead, the aging of our population implies that we should invest massively in raising the productivity of today's children, not just for their sake, but on behalf of the elderly of the next century as well.

The most recent proposal for this end springs from *Can America Afford to Grow Old? Paying for Social Security and Medicare* by Henry Aaron, Barry Bosworth and Gary Burtless. This 1988 publication is remarkable first for signalling the end of a long denial phase within mainstream liberalism over the future of these two programs. Its authors frankly acknowledge, and express concern for, the mounting burdens that Social Security and Medicare may impose on the next century's workers in the absence of adequate capital formation and investment.

Yet once the challenge to our future presented by debt and demographics is acknowledged, the hard part, of course, still remains. The economic definition of investment is deferred consumption. But whose consumption should we defer, and by what method? Granted the over-arching importance of increased capital formation in an aging society, how exactly should that capital be deployed and by whom?

To these questions, Aaron and his co-authors seem to have a straightforward answer. Today's working-aged Americans and their children should bear the sacrifice in consumption. Specifically, the authors examine the effects of a large buildup of the Social Security trust funds—financed entirely through increased taxes rather than reduced benefits. This, they argue, coupled with a substantial reduction in the government's overall budget deficits, will allow the trust funds to begin buying back the outstanding national debt held by the public, thereby increasing the pool of capital available for private investment. Reducing public debt, they remind us, raises the nation's savings rate just as surely as if the American people as a whole simply put more money in the bank. In the event the entire national debt were eventually refinanced through higher payroll taxes, the authors advise that the Social Security Administration invest in securities issued by Federal Government agencies or by private organizations such as the Federal National Mortgage Association that issue securities backed by Federal guarantees.

This agenda is far from radical. Indeed, the 1983 Amendments to the Social Security Act are widely interpreted to call for something like its enactment. Under current law, payroll taxes are set in excess of the amount needed to fund current Social Security benefits. Younger Americans are asked to believe that by paying these extra taxes, which Social Security invests in government bonds, they are in effect pre-paying the cost of their future benefits under the program. In essence, the authors are asking simply that the government continue to pursue this strategy, only more rigorously, and under conditions that might allow it to work.

Foremost among those conditions, as the authors correctly point out, is that the government immediately and substantially reduce its overall budget deficits. This prerequisite raises the first, and certainly the most obvious, obstacle to the plan's success, even assuming its many other practical as well as moral and theoretical problems could be overcome.

The authors rightly protest the government's current practice of using the Social Security trust funds to underwrite each year's recurring budget deficits. This practice is at best futile and at worst harmful to the extent that it masks the true size of each year's new deficit. Social Security cannot possibly contribute to an increase in the nation's saving rate if the government as a whole continues to borrow faster than the trust funds can absorb the debt with any surplus revenue.

So the deficits must be substantially eliminated for the plan to begin to work even at the level of theory. Yet, as a matter of practical politics, levying extra Social Security taxes cannot help but stiffen the public's resistance to any additional tax increases, such as those that would still be needed to balance the general operations budget.

This is a simple point, but one that is extremely important to the politics of deficit reduction. Indeed, the dramatic rise in payroll taxes since the early 1970s may go a long way toward explaining the rebellion against all other forms of taxation that has brought us first Reagan and now Bush. Raising payroll taxes still more, for whatever purpose, will leave the voters just that much less able or willing to sacrifice for other causes, including not just deficit reduction, but public investment of all forms. Since payroll taxes are highly regressive, the burden would be particularly great on low-income workers. The working poor would surely come to believe that this form of liberalism had become, at least for them, very expensive indeed.

At the same time, the prerequisite reduction in the government's overall budget deficits will be extremely difficult to achieve—many would say impossible—if the huge fraction of government spending now consumed by Social Security benefits remains off-limits to budget cuts—as the authors presume. If even the richest Social Security recipients are excused from the required, general sacrifice in consumption, other programs will have to be cut that much more deeply, and other taxes raised that much higher.

Moreover, no matter how the government keeps its books, this fiscal reality will become ever more difficult to escape in the future, as the aging of the population and rising medical costs conspire to drive up aggregate Social Security spending even in the absence of any new or more liberal individual benefits. Frankly, without benefit cuts, we will be lucky if we can raise payroll taxes fast enough just to keep up with the compounding annual cost of Medicare—which is now but one mild recession away from instant insolvency—let alone be able to raise any more funds from the public for deficit reduction, much less for repurchase of the outstanding national debt.

But let us suppose that by some combination of higher taxes and reduced spending, the government can and will balance its overall budget even without cutting Social Security. And let us suppose further that at this point, a majority of American workers will agree to paying still more Social Security taxes so that the system is able not only to keep up with its mounting current liabilities but also to begin purchasing all government bonds now held by private investors.

Obviously, all this would entail an enormous sacrifice on the part of today's working generation. If all went according to plan, we would be simultaneously paying the full current cost of government through taxation rather than deficit spending, while also refinancing all previous government deficits out of our own consumption, while finally, through Social Security and Medicare, continuing to support the consumption of the current elderly—regardless of need—on a pay-as-you-go basis. If it all worked, our children might be very grateful, indeed—as well as our parents. But will it work, and should we try?

The first large question, which the authors freely acknowledge, is the plan's possible effect on how much individual Americans decide to save on their own. Here, humility is in order, for the psychology of saving remains a subject about which virtually no two economists agree.

But this we can say as a matter of mathematical certainty: any increase in the payroll tax—for whatever purpose—will straightforwardly reduce the disposable income of working Americans, and to that extent reduce their ability, if not necessarily their proclivity, to save for themselves.

We do not know how much these Americans might save in any event. But we do know that every dollar they contribute to the Social Security Administration is a dollar they cannot possibly save for their own purposes—whether for a downpayment on a house, for their children's education, or most ironically, for their own retirement. Similarly, we know that higher payroll taxes will leave employers with less funds available for investment, while also reducing their incentives to hire and their ability to raise wages.

At the very least then, we cannot assume that every extra dollar contributed to the Social Security trust fund will bring an extra dollar in national saving, regardless of how the government uses the funds. Indeed, we must at least embrace the possibility that any increase in payroll taxes will cause Americans to save much less than they otherwise would, especially since the government meanwhile would be assuring Americans that by paying such a tax they would be reducing their need to provide otherwise for their retirement.

But again, let us give the authors the benefit of the doubt and suppose that their plan would not lead to any substantial reduction in private saving. Next comes a problem of a much more fundamental nature: What exactly happens when the Social Security Administration uses payroll taxes to buy back Treasury bonds from the public? Would this transaction be of any real benefit to future generations, or could it actually worsen the burden on the next generation?

One cause of concern is the widespread expectation among Americans, encouraged by government for over fifty years, that whatever funds they "contribute" to Social Security through their payroll taxes they will eventually receive back from the system, with interest. The plan would be much easier to analyze if, for example, it called for using the federal income tax, or any revenue source besides payroll taxes, to purchase government bonds now held by the public. This would be a story with an end in sight. True, we would never know to what extent the imposition of new taxes might have depressed economic growth and private savings. But we could be sure that the sums paid to private investors for their bonds would at least in part have become available for private investment. And at the same time, we could be sure the government would not, in the process, have created any new long-term liabilities.

But the question becomes much more complicated when payroll taxes are used for such a purpose. Payroll taxes are unlike all other forms of Federal revenue in that those who pay them at least perceive that they are purchasing an "earned right" to future benefits. Under current law, Social Security beneficiaries receive back an average 2.5 times the value of their original "investment" in Social Security, while Medicare recipients are entitled to 12 to 14 times the value of their previous taxes. For this reason, revenues previously collected through the payroll tax have obviously turned out to be, in reality, accrued, long-term liabilities now coming due—a relationship that might have been better appreciated had the government used an accrual system of accounting. While Congress obviously can and has cut the rate of return promised to future beneficiaries, the very process of collecting payroll taxes still creates at least a righteous expectation on the part of today's taxpayers that they also will receive their money back and more.

This in itself should caution us against using payroll taxes for any purpose other than paying current benefits. Today's taxpayers are paying an unprecedented proportion of their income to Social Security and Medicare; the more they pay in, the more benefits they will see themselves as having earned, and the more they will prevail on Congress to act accordingly. If not in a legal sense, then in a moral, political, and cultural dimension, revenues collected through what are perceived to be Social Security and Medicare "contributions" create claims on the next generation's wealth, in a way that income taxes and other taxes do not. Put more simply, for all these reasons and more, Congress is unlikely to resist spending any surplus that might appear on Social Security's books. As the power of the Gray Lobby compounds with the aging of the population, the pressure to raid the trust funds to satisfy the elderly of the moment can only increase.

But again, let us suppose that this obstacle to the plan's success can be overcome. We are now left with the purely theoretical question of whether the envisioned capital flows within the trust fund would be of any real benefit to the future. Here, the central point is that the plan calls not for the elimination of the national debt, but for a change in its ownership. The Social Security trust funds would purchase all Treasury bonds currently held by private investors. When that transaction was complete, the U.S. Treasury, and by extension future taxpayers, would still owe the principal and interest on these bonds, only the debt would now be payable to the Social Security Administration rather than to private sector investors.

An analogy from ordinary life is the experience of having one's mortgage sold by one bank to another. You still owe on your house, you just send the check to a different address. A closer, although still not perfect, comparison might be if your father, having already squandered the family fortune and worried about his support in old age, then scrimped and saved to buy the mortgage he left on you on the family farm. In the process, he might have done his part to raise the nation's saving rate higher than it otherwise would have been, and have thereby might even have marginally improved the economy while also enhancing his own prospects for retirement. But you would still be stuck with the same old debt.

What then changes under the plan? The current generation certainly pays extra taxes during its working years in order to allow Social Security to purchase the national debt, but does the next generation gain a corresponding increase in its standard of living? Perhaps, if the government has meanwhile refrained from further borrowing; if the required increase in payroll taxes has not been subtracted from private saving and has not depressed economic growth; and if Congress has refrained from spending the trust funds' assets on old age benefits or other forms of public consumption. Under these conditions, a larger pool of saving would certainly become available to the private sector than if we continued on our present spendthrift course. And if this pool of saving were invested productively, it might actually render the next generation richer than it otherwise would be.

But viewed from a generational equity perspective, this would hardly look like an act of stewardship. Remember, under the plan, the national debt is not paid down—as it might be—only refinanced. In that event, future taxpayers will still be liable for a debt they didn't create. Moreover, they will owe the money to a program whose prime beneficiaries will be members of the previous generation, on whose watch much of the debt was incurred in the first place.

Members of that generation, of course, would have made a large sacrifice in consumption under the plan, by paying extra taxes throughout the remainder of their working lives. But by doing so, they would by and large simply have made the national debt formally payable to themselves as future Social Security and Medicare beneficiaries. In effect, they will have taken Social Security's current unfunded liabilities and converted them into bonded debt, for which the next generation will be liable, regardless of its ability to pay.

To finance the aging of our population, we must save and invest more as a nation. This could be accomplished straightforwardly, and with little risk of unintended consequences, by simply mandating that individuals save more toward their retirement—with wealthier citizens compelled to save a greater share of their income than the poor. Certainly that is no less coercive than raising the payroll tax again across the board, or as hard on low-income workers and their employers. Nor would it leave the current working generation's resulting nest egg for retirement in the hands of a Congress dominated by the political power of the current elderly. Finally, unlike our current Individual Retirement Accounts and private pension plans, such a mandated saving program would not contribute to the deficits through forgone revenue. If we can mandate an increase in the minimum wage, we can mandate an increase in the saving rate as well, and we should.

At the same time, we must cope with the challenge of an aging society from the other side as well. Today, by virtually every measure of economic status, children as a group are a far more needy population than persons age 65 and over. Yet our current system literally taxes hundreds of thousands of young families beneath the poverty line, even as it redistributes roughly a fifth of its revenue to families having independent annual income of $20,000 or more. Even if the system was clearly solvent in the long term, we would have reason to question its increasingly regressive features. As it is, the system perversely helps undermine its own solvency by transferring resources from children and workers desperately in need of human investment to affluent seniors who are not.

Finally, we must frankly admit that, as the population ages rapidly in the next century, no amount of investment in the next generation will guarantee our continued ability to subsidize seniority per se, especially if we define seniority as beginning at an age when most people have 20 percent or more of their lifespan still in front of them. If we are to avoid the risk of encumbering the next generation with staggering Social Security and especially Medicare costs, we must reform these programs so that they insure against the possibility that any of us—through bad luck or poor health—may become needy in old age, rather than against the increasingly likely event that we will simply live to be at least age 62. Either that or a dramatic increase in the retirement age must be on the table as we struggle for a way to meet the needs not just of current senior citizens, but of the next century's elderly as well, without unjustly burdening the young.

DISCUSSION

Robert Kuttner*

I WANT TO CONGRATULATE THE FOUNDERS OF THE NATIONAL Academy of Social Insurance for both an inspired idea and good marketing. The name "National Academy of Social Insurance" reminds us that there is an issue of public philosophy here, that the whole idea of social insurance, put forward in the 1930s in this country, is a philosophical notion that a polity has a social as well as a market aspect to it. That is what we have to keep at the forefront.

I am also delighted that The Brookings Institution in the last few months has put out not one but two books that defend and expand social insurance: Alice Rivlin and Josh Weiner advocate that social insurance be expanded to cover long-term health care. Now, Henry Aaron, Barry Bosworth, and Gary Burtless not only defend social insurance but propose using it to, you should pardon the expression, socialize saving.

I strongly support the idea of segregating the Social Security budget from the operating budget because this separation brings four distinct benefits: First, it anchors the Social Security program fiscally. Second, it produces a higher saving rate. Third, it has the ideological benefit of demonstrating that you do not have to make the rich richer and the poor poorer in order to increase the national saving rate. A million-dollar increment to a Social Security trust fund adds just as much to the national saving stock as a million-dollar tax break for Pete Peterson. Too many of us on the liberal side gave away too much to the supply- siders eight years ago when we speculated that we have to sacrifice some equity to get some growth. This demonstrates that we do not, in a very powerful way.

Fourth, this proposal helps anchor the baby boom generation in the Social Security system, thereby helping to refute the generational-equity view of the world. Removing Social Security from the budget squarely

---

* Economics correspondent, *The New Republic.*

poses three choices that have been obscured in the current budget debate. We can continue the current fiscal irresponsibility and undercut Social Security for the long term; we can shortchange other spending needs; or we can raise taxes. If you take Social Security off budget, it is very difficult to avoid coming to terms with the reality that there is going to have to be a hefty progressive tax increase, not a token tax increase or a regressive increase in the gasoline tax. That is going to cause some discomfort in Congress, but I think it is very useful because it is economically necessary, not only for the health of Social Security but for the health of the economy.

So, I think the Aaron-Bosworth-Burtless book and Aaron's paper are well turned and well timed, and I think that even though the book downplays the implication, which is not just higher payroll taxes in the year 2000 and beyond, but rather a hefty tax increase now. With regard to Phil Longman, I wonder if he has moved to Florida out of masochism or as a deliberate way of stoking himself into a white heat as he sees these greedy geezers cavorting on the beaches with their ill-gotten Social Security checks.

I have long suspected and suggested that the so-called generational-equity school is essentially an ideological critique masquerading as a generational critique. Longman's paper makes that clear. He begins by congratulating Henry Aaron, somewhat tongue in cheek, I think, for recognizing that Social Security is, indeed, in fiscal trouble. But, of course, Aaron says nothing of the sort. What Aaron says is that Social Security is quite healthy and that the rest of the budget deficit is irresponsibly poaching on Social Security. He says that we have to do something now about the deficit in the rest of the budget, and that it might be a good idea in the next century to increase payroll taxes slightly so that the Social Security surplus does not just disappear after thirty years when the baby boom generation is fully retired, but remains as a permanent source of social saving that can permanently add to America's saving supply.

Longman makes the fair point that there might be a more equitable way of doing this than the payroll tax, and on this score I agree with him. I think President Roosevelt's Committee on Economic Security was right in calling for general revenues to supplement payroll taxes. This argument gains force if we use Social Security reserves to increase national saving.

Longman also suggests that Aaron is really advocating that today's working-aged Americans and their children should bear the sacrifice in consumption in order to increase the saving rate, and that government, ominously, should decide what to do with the resulting pool of saving.

Again, let us separate the generational critique from the ideological critique. Any increase in current saving depresses current consumption, whether it is voluntary as per the Longman plan or coercive as per the Aaron plan. The philosophical question is whether the saving rate is to be increased, socially or via market incentive, or through mandatory private saving.

Longman proposes mandated saving of the same fraction of income for their retirement, by wealthy and poor alike. This proposal is both more radical and more coercive than the call for large Social Security surpluses, but also less efficient. If some individual did not save enough or made bad investment choices and is destitute in retirement, society is still going to have to pick up the pieces one way or another. And, of course, that possibility brings us back to the original logic of social insurance, to require a collective Social Security program so that even if people are improvident, the money is there when they retire, and society does not have to pay the cost of their improvidence.

We also have the old favorite red herring of social insurance depressing saving rates, which I thought Dean Leimer and Selig Lesnoy disposed of in that wonderfully satisfying episode with Marty Feldstein. Furthermore, countries with more generous systems of social insurance than ours have, nonetheless, had much higher saving rates than our own. The argument has been proven that this approach, on balance, would not depress the aggregate saving rate.

What we have here at bottom is not really a debate about old versus young but a far older and more straightforward debate about laissez-faire versus a mixed economy and about market provision versus social insurance.

I wrote a piece in *The New Republic* in 1985 called "The Patrimony Society" pointing out that most intergenerational income transfers, after all, take place within the family. The generation slightly senior to mine amassed a lot of wealth, but, thanks to the almost non-existence of inheritance taxes, most of that wealth is going to be passed on to a segment of the baby boom generation. The real inequity in society is that many people, young and old, are struggling at the margins of economic life, while other people are living very high on the hog, at eighty or at forty.

The real issue is, will we support the principle of social insurance and, if so, how much should we pay for it? One tip-off to the fact that the generational-equity lobby really is an ideological assault disguised as generational solicitude is the fact that you rarely hear them saying, "Let's cut back social insurance for the old so that we can expand social insurance for the young."

Typically the statement is, "Let's cut back social insurance for the old so that we can cut the tax burden of the young and increase the relative role played by market, as opposed to social, provision of income." That is a perfectly defensible, straightforward position that unfortunately commands a current majority in America. But I would rather have it straight than have it filter through some concern for young people who are being made to pay too heavy a share of the tax burden.

One other point. A British sociologist, Julian LeGrand, pointed out that the National Health Service in Britain was really a net transfer from the poor to the middle class. Although the per capita use of the National Health Service was about the same in each social class, the poor were twice as medically needy as the rich, so, therefore, the rich were getting twice the intensity of usage of the poor. But where else in society are the rich only twice as rich as the poor?

There is a logic to social insurance. The real debate is how big a portion of the total economic pie it should claim. How do we go about expanding it to people who are not just old? The only reason the elderly are such an obvious target of assault is that they are the only group among us that has suceeded in building a real program of social insurance. I would rather see us talking about how we extend that umbrella to the young, without going broke in the process, and how we pay for the whole thing equitably.

DISCUSSION

John B. Shoven *

THE PAPER BY HENRY AARON, BASED ON HIS RECENT BOOK with Barry Bosworth and Gary Burtless, is valuable reading for anyone concerned about the long-run performance of the U.S. economy.

My role as a discussant is made more difficult by the fact that I fully agree with the paper's main point. The United States is not saving enough, and that lack will affect the well-being of future generations. A few statistics describe the general picture. U.S. net investment is currently about 6 percent of GNP. This rate of investment will enable the capital stock to grow about 2 percent per year. Because growth of the labor force will be slower than in recent decades, potential GNP will grow slowly, perhaps 2 or 2.5 percent per year, over the next decade and beyond.

Slowly growing potential GNP is only part of the story, however, and not the worst part. Half to two-thirds of the net investment is currently being financed abroad, which means that future workers may be forced to send a substantial amount of product abroad in order to service foreign debt. They also certainly will be forced to share a larger fraction of GNP with a substantially enlarged elderly population. Foreign financiers and the elderly are going to put the working population in the years 2010 to 2040 in a squeeze. Workers of that period may not enjoy significantly higher real, after-tax wage rates than do workers today. Since after-tax real wages have risen little in the past twenty years, we may experience a fifty-year stretch (roughly from 1970 to 2020) with little growth in real after-tax wages. Such a record would contrast sharply with the U.S. experience from 1940 through 1975 and with late twentieth century experience in such countries as Japan or Korea.

* Professor of Economics, Stanford University.

One thing that we could do now to ease the situation is increase domestic saving and curtail foreign loans. However, the medicine will not be pleasant. Simply to stop accumulating additional foreign obligations will require that consumption decline (relative to GNP) by 4 to 5 percent. Terminating foreign borrowing would require low growth in per capita real consumption for an extended period, perhaps as long as ten years. Increased saving is achievable, however: in the 1960s, the United States saved almost 9 percent of GNP, rather than the 2 to 3 percent of the past couple of years.

Based on his paper and book, I think it is fair to say that Henry Aaron and I agree on the above general diagnosis, even if it is bleak. We also agree that Social Security is basically in sound financial shape and that it is not a major part of the national saving problem. I probably would not go as far as he does on this point, however. When we have a general inadequacy of saving, any contribution would improve things, even if it came from a quarter which is already in pretty good shape. We would be better off if Social Security were truly in balance over the seventy-five year horizon rather than the sixty-year horizon as it now stands.

I also believe that Henry Aaron goes a little overboard in downplaying the importance of demographic factors and the "horrible ratios." The fact is that they are important. There are at least three ways to run a Social Security system: pay-as-you-go financing (where tax rates are set and the benefits are simply parcelled out from tax receipts); an unfunded defined-benefit system (where benefits are set and tax rates are adjusted to bring in the necessary revenues); and a partially prefunded defined-benefit system (where future benefits are anticipated and at least partially prefunded). The various systems impose different generational burdens. Consider, for example, the impact of a bulge in the population (a single, very numerous cohort). With a pay-as-you-go Social Security system, the generation before the population bulge does very well (reaps a windfall gain), whereas the bulge generation does relatively poorly. With an unfunded defined benefit plan, the incidence of the burden of the population bulge is shifted one generation. Now the numerous cohort does very well and the next or following cohort does poorly. This just illustrates that demographics and plan design interact in important ways.

The United States changed the financing of Social Security from an unfunded, defined-benefit system, and with the 1983 reforms, it is now a partially prefunded system. In fact, Henry Aaron characterizes it as conforming to a principle whereby each generation or cohort pays its own way ("pays its dues"). This switch in plan design alone would transfer the burden of the large baby boom elderly population from the next generation to the baby boom generation itself. The only problem is that while the baby boom generation has promised to shoulder more of the burden of its own retirements, it has simultaneously been on a consumption and borrowing binge. On net, it has not done future workers any favors.

The facts that we have switched to a partially prefunded system, and that the baby boom generation is going to bear more of the burden of its own retirement, are reflected both in a higher Social Security tax rate than would be required by an unfunded scheme and in the shorter retirements created by the scheduled increase in the age at which unreduced benefits may be claimed (loosely, the "normal retirement age"). The net effect of these changes is that the cohort as a whole will "earn" only a 2 percent real rate of return rather than the roughly 6 percent social rate of return on capital.

Switching to a partially prefunded system was a good idea. I would favor asking the generation before that of the baby boom to contribute to the extra costs of the system. I would do that by accelerating the rise in the "normal retirement age." The increase could begin as early as 1996 and could go steadily up by one month per year for twenty-four years. Benefits of anyone currently near retirement would be affected little if at all. However, such a step would contribute to increasing national saving, the number one priority.

My view is that national saving must be encouraged at all levels. Private saving needs to be pushed through both political leadership and incentives. Government dissaving needs to be eliminated both by cutting government consumption and by increasing taxes. In the latter category, I would include taxing all Social Security benefits received by those with adequate income and perhaps increasing gasoline taxes.

The fact is that the United States needs to save and invest more in the future. Future workers are going to face an unprecedented burden unless we do something. The primary problem is our inappropriate fiscal policy. As Henry Aaron emphasizes, the problem is not Social Security.

CONGRESS AND THE PUBLIC: CONVERGENT AND DIVERGENT OPINIONS ON SOCIAL SECURITY

Fay Lomax Cook *

T ALK ABOUT THE SOCIAL SECURITY CRISIS VARIOUSLY defined has been widespread for at least the last ten years. Three definitions of this crisis exist. Before 1983, newspapers headlined a fiscal crisis, the impending bankruptcy of the Social Security trust funds. More recently, the mass media have identified the large surplus now building up in the Social Security trust funds as a new cause for alarm.

A second alleged crisis is the concern, particularly among young adults, that Social Security will not be there when they retire.[1] Many commentators infer from these findings that young people do not support Social Security and are not willing to continue to pay Social Security taxes.

Third, some commentators find a crisis of politics in what they see as a political stalemate, constrained on the one side by policymakers' fear of elderly interest groups and on the other side by the budget deficit. Light[2],

* Associate Professor of Education and Social Policy, Northwestern University

The research for this paper was funded by a grant from the Ford Foundation. Edith J. Barrett collaborated on much of the research on which the paper is based. Bernice Neugarten deserves thanks for many thoughtful and helpful suggestions.

[1] Louis Harris and Associates, *Aging in the Eighties: America in Transition*, Washington, D.C., The National Council on Aging, 1981. Yankelovich, Skelly and White, Inc., *A Fifty-Year Report Card on the Social Security System: The Attitudes of the American Public*, Washington, D.C., American Association of Retired Persons, 1985. Timothy Harper, "Americans Want Social Security, But Don't Have Much Faith In It," Associated Press, New York, 1982.

[2] Paul Light, *Artful Work: The Politics of Social Security Reform*, New York, Random House, 1985.

for example, thinks that members of Congress set a trap for themselves
when they claimed that the 1983 Social Security Amendments solved all
Social Security problems for the indefinite future, thereby obviating the
need for further action. In truth, says Light, periodic legislative adjustment
will always be necessary and Social Security will never escape budgetary
pressure.[3]

This paper reports the results of a study that probes the latter two
definitions of the crisis of Social Security. First, it reports on support for
Social Security, among the public in general and young adults in particular,
and examines whether a crisis of support really exists. Second, it reports on
attitudes toward Social Security among members of the U.S. House of
Representatives, considers whether a crisis of politics exists from the perspective of the Representatives, and if so, asks wherein the crisis lies.
Further, it examines the extent to which Representatives' levels of support
are different from the public's and why these differences might exist.

Few studies have measured congressional opinions and compared them
to public opinion. Instead, scholars usually infer opinions of members of
Congress from voting records and compare these records to the opinions of
either their constituents or the public as a whole. The objective is to
determine whether members of Congress reflect the views of their constituents or the nation.

The resulting descriptions are problematic for two reasons: First, most
bills before Congress "bundle" many policy decisions into one wide-ranging
measure that requires a yes or no vote as a whole, an all or nothing choice.[4]
Second, bills before Congress and questions on opinion surveys seldom
share the same wording; thus, comparisons between congressional votes
and public opinion are difficult to make. In the study reported here, the
wording of the questions put to members of the House of Representatives
is the same as the questions asked the public. Thus, the expressed preferences of Representatives and of the public can be compared.

Since the mid 1970s, commentators have found growing worries about
Social Security.[5] In 1981, Louis Harris and Associates found that 68 percent
of Americans aged 18 to 54 had "hardly any" confidence that the present

[3] Ibid. p. 237.

[4] Roger H. Davidson, "The New Centralization on Capital Hill," Paper presented at the
Annual Meeting of the Midwest Political Science Association, Chicago, IL 1988.

[5] Leonard Goodwin and Joseph Tu, "The Social Psychological Basis for Public Acceptance
of the Social System: The Role for Research in Public Policy Formation," *American
Psychologist*, 1975, pp. 875–83.

Social Security system would be able to pay them benefits when they retired, 23 percent had "some" confidence, and only 6 percent had a "great deal" of confidence.[6] NBC News/Associated Press in 1982 also found low levels of confidence, especially among the young: 85 percent of young adults aged 18 to 24 and 89 percent of those aged 25 to 34 said that they had "only a little confidence" or "no confidence" that Social Security would have the money to pay benefits upon their retirement.[7] In 1985, Yankelovich again found low levels of confidence in the future of Social Security among young adults.[8]

Dramatic improvements have occurred since the early 1960s in the well-being of the elderly, due primarily to the introduction of Medicaid, Medicare, Supplemental Security Income (SSI), increases in Social Security benefits, and Social Security cost of living increases (COLAs). Some commentators have speculated that these improvements and the deterioration in the economic status of children have undermined public willingness to pay into a system that aids all elderly citizens regardless of their financial need. Phillip Longman, a former official in Americans for Generational Equity (AGE), notes that "more than $10 billion in Social Security checks will go to elderly households whose income already exceeds $25,000 annually."[9]

Despite such criticisms, public opinion polls have found declines only in confidence in the Social Security system, and not in public willingness to support continuation of the system.[10] Most of the relevant research to date has measured support in terms of the percentage of respondents who oppose cuts in federal spending for Social Security[11] and in terms of beliefs about whether the government should spend more, less, or about the same amount of money on Social Security.[12] No previous surveys exist that ask respondents how far they think they would go behaviorally to show their

---

[6] Louis Harris and Associates, op. cit.

[7] Timothy Harper, op. cit.

[8] Yankelovich, Skelly and White, Inc., op. cit.

[9] Phillip Longman, "Taking America to the Cleaners," *The Washington Monthly*, 1982, pp. 24–30.

[10] Robert Y. Shapiro and Tom W. Smith, "The Polls: Social Security," *Public Opinion Quarterly*, August 1985.

[11] Harris and Associates, March 1980, January 1981, August 1981, September 1981, August 1982; and Gallup Polls, January 1981, January, 1983.

[12] Robert Y. Shapiro and Tom W. Smith, op. cit., pp. 561–72.

support—for example, write their representatives in Congress or pay higher taxes. In addition, no large-scale national surveys have tried to find out why the public feels as it does about Social Security.

Public support for any social welfare program may be related to at least four programmatic attributes. First is whether or not the program is perceived by the public as benefiting society.[13] Second is the extent to which it is seen to operate efficiently—that is, without fraud and abuse.[14] Third is whether it is seen to maximize the self-sufficiency and independence of its recipients.[15] Fourth is whether it is seen to create dependency—that is, to make people dependent on the benefits they receive and unable to get along on their own.[16]

Attributes of the recipients of a program may also be important. These characteristics include: perception of the recipients' need,[17] the availability of alternative sources of help,[18] the recipients' desire for independence,[19] the recipients' responsibility for their plight,[20] and the recipients' prudence in using benefits.[21] This chapter reports new information on both the extent to which such perceptions explain levels of support and the actions

---

[13] J.M. Romanyshyn, *Social Welfare: Charity to Justice*, New York, Random House, 1971. Robert B. Reich, *Tales of a New America*, New York, Random House, 1987.

[14] Charles D. Samuelson and David M. Messick, "Inequalities in Access to and Use of Shared Resources in Social Dilemmas," *Journal of Personality and Social Psychology*, 1986, pp. 960–67.

[15] Fay Lomax Cook, *Who Should Be Helped? Public Support for Social Services*, Beverly Hills, CA, Sage, 1979.

[16] Charles Murray, *Losing Ground: American Social Policy 1950–1980*, New York, Basic, 1984.

[17] Fay Lomax Cook, op. cit.

[18] Ibid.

[19] Robert E. Lane, *Political Ideology*, New York, The Free Press, 1962. James R. Kluegal and Eliot R. Smith, *Beliefs About Inequality: Americans' Views of What Is and What Ought to Be*, New York, Aldine de Gruyter, 1986.

[20] Leonard Berkowitz and D.H. Connor, "Success, Failure, and Social Responsibility," *Journal of Personality and Social Psychology*, 1966, pp. 664–69. M.J. Lerner, D.T. Miller, and J.G. Holmes, "Deserving and the Emergence of Forms of Justice," *Advances in Experimental Social Psychology*. Vol. 9, Equity Theory: Toward a General Theory of Social Interaction, New York, Academic, 1976, pp. 134–162. Edited by Leonard Berkowitz and Elaine Walster.

[21] Gerald S. Leventhal, Thomas Weiss, and Richard Buttrick, "Attribution of Value, Equity, and the Prevention of Waste in Reward Allocation," *Journal of Personality and Social Psychology*, 1973, pp. 276–86.

which members of the public report they will take to support Social Security.

Research Design

This examination of public and congressional opinion about Social Security is part of a larger study[22] that measured levels and determinants of support for seven social welfare programs and examined how decisions were made about selecting social groups (e.g., children, elderly, etc.) and the programs to help them. Two separate surveys were conducted, one of the public and a second of members of the U.S. House of Representatives.

Trained interviewers from Northwestern University's Survey Research Laboratory conducted telephone interviews during the fall of 1986 with 1,209 U.S. adults who were randomly selected to represent the continental United States population aged 18 and over.[23] All 1,209 respondents answered a series of questions to measure support for Social Security and six other social welfare programs. A subsample of 495 respondents also answered additional questions in more depth about their level of support for Social Security and their perceptions of the program and its beneficiaries. Appendix Table 1 shows that the 1986 sociodemographic characteristics of the U.S. public closely resembled those of respondents in both the entire sample and the subsample.

Between May and August, 1986, I interviewed fifty-eight members of the U.S. House of Representatives in person. The sample included thirty-four

---

[22] Fay Lomax Cook, Edith J. Barrett, Susan J. Popkin, Ernesto A. Constantino, and Julie E. Kaufman, "Convergent Perspectives on Social Welfare Policy: The Views from the General Public, Members of Congress, and AFDC Recipients." Evanston, Illinois, Center for Urban Affairs and Policy Research, 1988.

[23] The interviews averaged approximately 45 minutes in length. The Survey Laboratory used a one-stage random digit dialing procedure to obtain a random sample of all U.S. households. Once connected to the household, interviewers used the "last-birthday" method, a probability method that requires the interviewer to speak with the person in the household who celebrated the most recent birthday. This procedure has been shown in past research to yield an unbiased sample without requiring time-consuming enumeration of household members. (See Charles T. Salmon and John Spicer Nichols, "The Next-Birthday Method of Respondent Selection." *Public Opinion Quarterly*, Vol. 47, 1983, pp. 270–276.) Excluding the non-eligible telephone numbers and those for which eligibility could not be determined, the response rate was 69 percent for totally completed interviews and 71 percent for completed and partially completed interviews. These percentages are comparable to response rates achieved in other telephone surveys. (See Salmon and Nichols, op. cit; Kluegal and Smith, op. cit. and Ronald Czaja, Johnny Blair and Jutta Sebestik "Respondent Selection in a Telephone Survey: A Comparison of Three Techniques." *Journal of Marketing Research*, Vol. 19, 1982, pp. 381–385.)

Representatives chosen randomly and twenty-four chosen because they were chairs (if Democratic) or ranking minority members (if Republican) of committees and subcommittees having jurisdiction over social welfare policy issues. These committees included the Appropriations Committee, Budget Committee, Ways and Means Committee, Education and Labor Committee, Energy and Commerce Committee, Select Committee on Aging, and Select Committee on Children, Family, and Youth.

Despite a letter of introduction from the chair of an influential committee, not all Representatives granted interviews. The response rate was 60 percent for the random sample—62 percent for Republicans and 59 percent for Democrats.[24] To replace the fourteen Representatives who were unable or refused to be interviewed, I sought interviews with fourteen others, all but one of whom completed an interview. Thus, the final random sample consists of thirty-four Representatives. The response rate for the purposive sample was 71 percent—59 percent for Republicans and 82 percent for Democrats—leaving a final purposive sample composed of twenty-four chairpersons and ranking minority members.[25] Appendix Table 2 compares selected sociodemographic and political characteristics of the actual membership of the House of Representatives in 1986 to the entire sample, weighted so that the purposive sample is in proportion to its actual size in the House. The sample mirrors very closely the composite membership of the House.[26]

---

[24] The reasons for refusals were similar—prolonged illness, absence from Washington due to family problems or campaigning for another office, or a "policy" never to grant interviews to researchers. (Some stated they'd been "burned" in the past.)

[25] The response rate for purposively sampled Republicans is very similar to that for Republicans in the random sample. However, the 82 percent rate of completion by Democratic chairpersons is considerably higher than for Democrats in the random sample. It is puzzling that Democratic committee leaders are so much more willing to be interviewed than both Republican leaders and Democratic Representatives in the random sample. We can only speculate that the reason is their greater interest, for the interviews revealed that they were extremely interested in the fact that someone was doing a study of this type and they hoped the results of the study could eventually be useful to them in their committee work.

[26] The percentages of Republicans (41.3 percent) and Democrats (58.6 percent) in the sample are almost identical to the actual percentages (41.8 percent and 58.1 percent, respectively). Also extremely close are age (a mean of 50.1 for our sample as compared to 49.7 for the House's total membership); length of time in Congress (a sample mean of 8.25 years as compared to 8.38); percent black (5.7 percent versus 4.6 percent); and comparisons of voting records using scores developed by the Children's Defense Fund, the National Council of Senior Citizens, Americans for Democratic Action, Americans for Constitutional Action, and the National Journal. Regional representation is also close. With respect to education, the sample has fewer members with master's and doctoral degrees than was found in the House's population, and it had more lawyers than would be expected.

Measures of Support

Responses to several questions measured support for Social Security. First, respondents in both the public sample and the sample of U.S. Representatives answered a question about whether they thought benefits should be increased, decreased, or maintained at their present levels after inflation was taken into account. So that support for Social Security could be compared to support for other social welfare programs, I included a similar question about Medicare, Medicaid, SSI, Food Stamps, Unemployment Compensation, and Aid to Families with Dependent Children (AFDC).

Second, the public answered four questions about the commitments that they would be willing to make to stand behind their preferences. The first concerned satisfaction with paying taxes. Interviewers asked: "In general, how satisfied are you with the fact that a part of every working person's income goes to support the Social Security program?" The second dealt with intensity of satisfaction or dissatisfaction. Respondents who expressed satisfaction were asked, "If you were told that spending for Social Security was going to be cut back, would you be strongly opposed, somewhat opposed, or indifferent?" Level of dissatisfaction was measured through the answer to the question: "If you were told that spending for Social Security was going to be expanded, would you be strongly opposed, somewhat opposed, or indifferent?" In addition, dissatisfied respondents were asked why they did not favor Social Security.

A third question concerned willingness to take action. Interviewers asked: "Would you sign a petition or write a letter to your Congressman expressing your feelings toward the cutback [your disapproval of the expansion]?" The final test of support was a question concerning willingness to make a monetary commitment. Interviewers asked: "In order to prevent the Social Security program from being cut back, would you be willing to have people pay no more Social Security taxes, $0.50 more for every $100 they already pay, $1.00 more for every $100 they already pay, or $2.00 more for every $100?" [Or "To show your disapproval of Social Security, would you like the program to be maintained at its current funding, be cut back by $0.50 for every $100 in Social Security taxes spent on it, be cut back by $1.00 for every $100 spent, or be cut back by $2.00 for every $100 spent?"] I created an overall measure of support (the "disposition to action scale") by adding these four measures together, with a score that ranged from −10 to +10.[27]

Finally, I sought to identify the factors that influence the public's support

---

[27] The measures fit well together as a scale (Cronbach's alpha = 0.88).

Table 1
Public Support for Increasing, Maintaining, or Decreasing
Benefits for Seven Social Welfare Programs

RESPONSES
Program Benefits Should Be:

	Increased[a] Percent	Maintained Percent	Decreased Percent	Mean Support Score[b]
Medicare N = 1198	67.6	29.9	2.5	2.65
Supplemental Security Income N = 1167	57.3	40.0	2.7	2.55
Social Security N = 1200	56.7	40.0	3.3	2.53
Medicaid N = 1170	47.1	46.3	6.6	2.40
Unemployment Compensation N = 1155	31.5	55.5	13.0	2.18
Aid to Families With Dependent Children N = 1170	32.6	51.9	15.5	2.17
Food Stamps N = 1132	24.6	51.0	24.4	2.00

[a] The mean scores on a 3-point scale range from 3 (increase) to 1 (decrease). Standard deviations range from 0.44 to 0.72.

[b] Mean support for Social Security is comparable to that for the Supplemental Security Income [Paired $\underline{T}(1152) = -0.33, p < .75$] but significantly lower than the mean support for Medicare [Paired $\underline{T}(1176) = -6.78, p < .001$]. It is significantly higher than support for Medicaid [Paired $\underline{T}(1155) = 5.83, p < .001$], Unemployment Compensation [Paired $\underline{T}$ $(1137) = 16.08, p < .001$], Aid to Families with Dependent Children [Paired $\underline{T}$ $(1150) = 15.94. p < .001$], and Food Stamps [Paired $\underline{T}(1115) = 22.09, p < .001$].

for Social Security by selecting several variables hypothesized to relate to support for social welfare programs or groups in general. To probe perceptions about the beneficiaries of Social Security, interviewers asked respondents whether they agree, somewhat agree, somewhat disagree, or disagree with statements about Social Security recipients' need ("Most people now receiving Social Security really need the assistance provided"); alternative sources of help ("Most people who get Social Security have no sources of income other than Social Security"); desire for independence ("Most people who get Social Security want to be independent and self-reliant"); responsibility for plight ("It's a person's own fault if he gets Social Security instead of private retirement funds"); and prudence ("Most people who get Social Security spend their money wisely"). To probe perceptions about the Social Security program, interviewers used similar agree-disagree statements to ask respondents the extent to which they see Social Security as a benefit to society, as helping beneficiaries become more independent, as creating dependency in its beneficiaries, and as a program where "cheating" occurs.

Since members of Congress are said to resist closed-ended questions, I asked them only a few, one of which was the question on support for increasing, maintaining, or decreasing benefits. To determine the reasons for their level of supportiveness, I simply asked in open-ended fashion why they took the particular position they did.

The Views of the Public

Levels of Support

Members of the public overwhelmingly favor maintaining or increasing Social Security benefits. Fifty-seven percent of the respondents in the public sample wanted Social Security benefits to be increased, 40 percent wanted benefits maintained, and only 3 percent wanted to see benefits decreased. Table 1 shows both the mean levels of support and the percentages of each response for the seven major social welfare programs. Mean support for Social Security is comparable to that for SSI and is significantly higher than support for Medicaid, Unemployment Compensation, AFDC, and Food Stamps. Medicare receives the highest support. One characteristic links the three programs with the highest support: Medicare, Social Security, and SSI all serve the elderly.

How willing are members of the public to back up their preferences? Willing enough to express satisfaction with paying Social Security taxes (Table 2). An impressive 82 percent of the respondents state they are satisfied that a portion of each working person's income goes to finance

Table 2
Public Support for Social Security:
Percent with Positive or Negative Beliefs Willing to Take Actions

		Percent in Age Group		
	All	18–34	35–49	50–64	65 +
Satisfied with paying Social Security Taxes	82	81	79	81	88
Of those satisfied,					
Opposed to spending cuts	90	86	91	91	97
Willing to write Congress member or sign a petition	77	72	77	82	86
Willing to pay higher taxes	71	73	75	74	59
Dissatisfied with paying Social Security taxes	18	19	21	19	12
Of those dissatisfied,					
Opposed to increases	60	59	58	78	44
Willing to write Congress member or sign petition	43	41	46	56	11
Willing to decrease taxes	27	30	31	34	11

Social Security. When questioned further about their degree of satisfaction, 90 percent say they would be opposed to any spending cutbacks in Social Security. Furthermore, those respondents who are satisfied say they would be willing to stand behind their beliefs: 77 percent said they would be willing to write a letter or sign a petition to their representative in Congress and 71 percent said they would pay higher taxes.[28]

---

[28] Although we have no way of knowing for certain whether the respondents would actually perform these acts, considerable evidence from other studies suggests two major conditions under which beliefs are closely related to behaviors: 1) when the beliefs are about behaviors and 2) when they are specific in their referent. (See M. Fishbein and I. Ajzen, *Belief, Attitude, Intention, and Behavior: An Introduction to Theory and Research,* Reading, MA: Addison-Wesley, 1975.) Two of the support measures are clearly behaviorally grounded, being based on the willingness to pay taxes and to sign petitions or write letters. Moreover, respondents were not asked their opinions about global social welfare programs (for example, "welfare") as in some attitude surveys. (See Tom W. Smith "That Which We

Dissatisfied respondents feel less strongly about their beliefs than do satisfied respondents. Only 43 percent would write letters or sign petitions, and only 27 percent want their taxes decreased. When those who were dissatisfied were asked why they did not want their taxes cut, 38 percent said they fear that Social Security will not be available for them when they retire. The remaining dissatisfied respondents have various grievances against the program, the most common being a belief that individuals could do better investing their own money in private pension plans (19 percent) and that too many people who are receiving benefits don't really need them (16 percent).

Young Respondents

Some commentors claim that younger adults are less satisfied with Social Security than older adults, primarily because the young perceive the program as failing and do not wish to pay into it for their future.[29] This assertion can be tested by examining the extent to which younger respondents are in fact less supportive than older respondents in the levels of benefits they favor and in their willingness to say they would act to help preserve the program.

The results in Table 2 do not support this view. A slightly larger proportion of elderly respondents are satisfied than are others, but no differences distinguish the three age groups under 65. The elderly are also more likely to be opposed to spending cutbacks and are more likely to report they would write a letter or sign a petition opposing cuts, but they are less likely to be willing to have Social Security taxes increased to avoid the cutback. Although the non-elderly are slightly less likely to be satisfied with paying Social Security taxes, those who are satisfied are willing to pay more taxes if necessary to avoid cutbacks. Furthermore, the youngest respondents, who will be financially supporting Social Security for the next generation, are no less supportive than are respondents closer to retirement age. None of the age differences is particularly striking. A majority of respondents in each age group is highly supportive of Social Security.

Call Welfare by Any Other Name Would Smell Sweeter: An Analysis of the Impact of Question Wording on Response Patterns," *Public Opinion Quarterly*, Vol. 51, Spring 1987, pp. 561–572.) Instead, they were asked questions about their willingness to act in support of a specific program, Social Security. According to Fishbein and Ajzen, such behaviorally grounded and referent specific measures are better predictors of support than more affect-laden measures of attitudes, although, of course, no measure perfectly predicts actual behavior.

[29] Phillip Longman, op. cit., pp. 24–30.

Table 3
Support for Social Security by Selected Respondent Characteristics

	Increase-Decrease Scale[a] N = 1209		Action Support Scale[b] N = 492	
	Mean	N	Mean	N
Total	2.53	(1200)	4.54[b]	(492)
Age				
18 to 34	2.53	(465)[c]	4.27	(198)
35 to 49	2.52	(331)	4.22	(126)
50 to 64	2.56	(225)	4.62	(94)
65 and over	2.54	(177)	5.69	(74)
Race				
Black	2.81	(111)***	5.43	(49)
White	2.51	(1032)	4.51	(423)
Gender				
Male	2.43	(517)***	3.93	(211)*
Female	2.51	(683)	4.98	(282)
Income				
Less than $5000	2.77	(58)***	5.67	(18)
$5,000 to $10,000	2.71	(118)	5.72	(39)
$10,000 to $20,000	2.64	(285)	5.11	(117)
$20,000 to $35,000	2.52	(323)	4.05	(128)
$35,000 to $50,000	2.40	(196)	4.32	(87)
$50,000 +	2.40	(220)	3.68	(81)

Table 3 provides additional evidence. It shows a breakdown by age of the mean responses on the increase-decrease scale and the disposition to action scale. Younger respondents appear no less supportive than do respondents aged 35 to 49 or 50 to 64. They are somewhat less supportive than the elderly, though the difference is not statistically significant. The similarity across age groups is especially striking when support is measured in terms of a desire to increase or maintain benefits: the mean support expressed by the 18 to 34 year olds (2.53) is not different from the support by the elderly

Table 3 (cont.)
Support for Social Security by Selected Respondent Characteristics

	Increase-Decrease Scale[a] N = 1209		Action Support Scale[b] N = 492	
	Mean	N	Mean	N
Political Ideology				
Very liberal	2.64	(55)	6.04	(27)*
Somewhat liberal	2.54	(392)	4.90	(143)
Moderate	2.46	(43)	4.50	(18)
Somewhat conservative	2.51	(552)	4.36	(243)
Very conservative	2.50	(101)	2.47	(34)
Party Identification				
Democrat	2.62	(513)***	5.17	(213)*
Independent	2.59	(246)	4.52	(103)
Republican	2.40	(412)	3.82	(165)

[a] Scores range from 3 (increase) to 1 (decrease).

[b] Scores range from −10 to +10.

[c] Analyses of variance, taking into consideration unequal cell size, were performed on each of the groups to test whether the means of the subgroups are reliably different from each other. Three asterisks represent a difference between their support scores of p < .001; two asterisks, p < .01; one asterisk, p < .05.

(2.54). With the disposition to action scale, the elderly are a bit more supportive than the others, but among the non-elderly there are no differences; none of the age differences is statistically significantly different from any other.

Other Demographic Differences

Black respondents are somewhat more supportive of Social Security than are white respondents, regardless of income. While low-income whites are more supportive than upper-income whites, black respondents are equally supportive at all income levels. The interaction between race and income also holds true when support is measured using the increase-decrease scale. Only one difference exists between the races on the subscales of the support measure; about 10 percent more black respondents than whites are willing to write letters and sign petitions to protest cutbacks (86 percent vs. 77 percent).

Women are more supportive of Social Security than are men. This finding holds true even when we control for race, age, and income. More women than men express satisfaction with the program but the intensity of support among those who express satisfaction is similar. Although men are less likely to be satisfied with paying taxes, those who are satisfied are just as willing as women to write letters and to pay higher taxes.[30]

Democrats are more supportive than Republicans; independents fall in between. Democrats are more satisfied than Republicans that every working individual pays Social Security taxes (86 percent vs. 78 percent); they are more opposed to spending cutbacks (92 percent vs. 85 percent); and they are more willing to write letters or sign petitions (84 percent vs. 71 percent). Given that a respondent is satisfied, however, Democrats and Republicans are almost equally willing to have their taxes increased (71 percent vs. 72 percent). Republicans may be less satisfied and less supportive overall, but when they are supportive they are as willing to stand behind their support with their tax dollars as are Democrats.

Respondents who label themselves politically liberal are more satisfied with paying Social Security taxes than those who consider themselves political conservatives. In fact, much of the difference in support between the political parties can be explained by the political ideology of the respondents. Democrats overall tend to be more supportive than Republicans, and a much larger proportion of Democrats consider themselves politically liberal (49 percent) than do Republicans (22 percent). Although liberal Democrats are the most supportive group, liberal Republicans are still relatively supportive.

Differences between sociodemographic groups account for very little of the variance in support scores. Age, sex, race, income, and education account for only 2.1 percent of the variance in support scores. Ideology and party affiliation explain 3.2 percent more of the variance in support. Thus, it appears that factors other than sociodemographic characteristics of the public must explain support for Social Security.

---

[30]Unlike Goodwin and Tu (1975), we find no significant differences between the support expressed by women with and without college education.

Table 4
Public Perceptions of Social Security Program and
Social Security Beneficiaries

Perceptions	% Agree	Percent Responding		
		% Somewhat Agree	% Somewhat Disagree	% Disagree
Perceived Program Characteristics				
"Society benefits from the program"	68.9	20.4	4.3	6.4
"Makes people dependent"	13.4	10.5	20.5	55.6
"Leads to independence"	57.5	21.3	9.8	11.4
"Many people cheat the program"	0.8	9.8	28.6	60.8
Perceived Beneficiary Characteristics				
"No alternative sources of income"	40.4	23.0	13.3	23.3
"Really need money"	60.9	27.6	6.5	5.0
"Want to be independent"	76.9	13.1	4.7	5.3
"Own fault in program"	16.2	9.1	15.6	59.1
"Spend benefits wisely"	68.1	21.3	6.0	4.6

Beliefs Related to Support

If age, other demographic characteristics, political ideology, and political affiliation do not explain support for Social Security, what does? This question may be addressed by looking at respondents' perceptions of the Social Security program and of Social Security recipients. Table 4 shows the distribution of responses on nine perception questions. Respondents have very positive images about both the program and its recipients. For the most part, respondents believe that Social Security helps most recipients become independent (79 percent) and that it benefits society as a whole (89 percent). On the other hand, they don't believe it makes recipients dependent (24 percent agreement). The respondents also perceive little abuse occurring in the program.

Table 4 shows that the image of Social Security recipients held by the majority of the public is one of prudent people who need the money and have few alternative sources of income. Moreover, the public believes that Social Security recipients want to be independent and self-sufficient and are not at fault for needing benefits.

In order to examine the extent to which these perceptions of the Social Security program and its recipients explain overall support for the program, I performed a path analysis.[31] The first column of Table 5 shows the path coefficients of the model when support for Social Security is predicted on the basis of the perception variables alone. Table 5 shows not only how much of the variance in support is explained but also which factors make the major contributions. The belief that society as a whole benefits from Social Security clearly outweighs all other factors. Other perceptions of the program add little to the prediction. Program characteristics that researchers have hypothesized to have an effect on support for social welfare programs in general—for example, perceptions of fraud and abuse and the extent to which a program makes its recipients dependent—explained little of the variation in support for Social Security.

Public perceptions of Social Security recipients are less important in explaining support for the program than are perceptions that the program is a benefit to society. Only the perception that recipients have no alternative sources of income other than Social Security is significantly and positively related to support.

---

[31] The LISREL causal modeling package was used to analyze the relationship between beliefs and support. LISREL allows us to account for less than perfect reliability in the measurement of the constructs under examination because multiple measures can be used to indicate a single construct. It has the added advantage of computing maximum likelihood estimates of the path coefficients, and these tend to be more precise than the traditional least squares estimates. Each belief, whether directed at the Social Security program or recipients, represented a single indicator—the attitude under question. On the other hand, the dependent variable, support for Social Security, is based on four indicators, the four components of the action support score. LISREL allows for these different measurement strategies. In interpreting the results, it is important to understand that it is difficult to deal with data in which positive responses greatly exceed negative ones, given the limitations of path analysis. Thus, taking into account the highly supportive responses of the public, the model does fairly well in explaining support ($R^2 = .27$).

Table 5

Predictors of Support for Social Security from Two Different LISREL Models

	Model With Perceptions Only[a]	Model With Sociodemographic Characteristics Added
Perceived Program Characteristics		
"Society benefits from the program"	.385***	.302***
"Makes people dependent"	−.088	−.082
"Leads to independence"	.052	.108*
"Many people cheat the program"	−.012	−.055
Perceived Recipient Characteristics		
"No alternative sources of income"	.133**	.121***
"Really need money"	.061	.082
"Want to be independent"	−.052	−.004
"Own fault in program"	−.028	−.013
"Spend benefits wisely"	−.010	.037
Demographic Characteristics		
Race (1 = Black; 0 = White)	n.a.	.151**
Age	n.a.	.040
Income	n.a.	−.034
Gender (1 = Female; 0 = Male)	n.a.	.028
Education	n.a.	−.018
Political Characteristics		
Liberalism	n.a.	.092*
Party (1 = Democrat; 0 = Repub., Indep.)	n.a.	.060
	$R^2 = 0.27$	$R^2 = 0.29$

[a] Path analyses were carried out to analyze the factors related to support for Social Security. The first analysis was based only on the respondents' perceptions of Social Security and Social Security beneficiaries. The resulting path coefficients are in column 1. The second analysis added respondents' characteristics to the other predictor variables. The resulting path coefficients are in column 2.

n.a. = not applicable

* = $p < .05$; ** = $p < .01$; *** = $p < .001$

Table 6
Comparison of U.S. Representatives and the General Public on Their Support for Benefits for Seven Major Social Welfare Programs

	Representatives Percent	General Public Percent	Difference[a]
Medicaid			
Increase	41.8	47.1	
Maintain	52.8	46.3	
Decrease	5.4	6.6	
Mean Support Score	(1) 2.36[b]	(4) 2.40	
AFDC			
Increase	32.7	32.6	
Maintain	58.7	51.9	
Decrease	8.2	15.5	
Mean Support Score	(2) 2.25	(6) 2.17	
Medicare			
Increase	32.4	67.6	
Maintain	55.6	29.9	
Decrease	10.9	2.5	
Means Tested	1.2	—	
Mean Support Score	(3) 2.22	(1) 2.65	**
SSI			
Increase	23.8	57.3	
Maintain	68.0	40.0	
Decrease	8.2	2.7	
Mean Support Score	(4) 2.16	(2) 2.55	**

The second column indicates that the only sociodemographic characteristics related to support for Social Security are the respondent's race (blacks are more supportive than whites) and position on the liberal-conservative scale. The demographic and political variables alone account for only 5 percent of the variance in support scores and add only 2 percent to the variance explained in support for Social Security.

In summary, it is clear that there appears to be no crisis of public support for Social Security among any groups within the public. Despite their concerns about its long term viability, young adults are satisfied that a portion of their income goes to support Social Security, and a majority are willing to spend higher taxes to preserve it. Among other demographic

Table 6 (cont.)
Comparison of U.S. Representatives and the General Public on Their Support for Benefits for Seven Major Social Welfare Programs

	Representatives Percent	General Public Percent	Difference[a]
Social Security			
Increase	11.7	56.7	
Maintain	85.5	40.0	
Decrease	0	3.3	
Means Tested	2.7	—	
Mean Support Score	(5) 2.12	(2) 2.53	**
Unempl. Comp.			
Increase	12.3	31.5	
Maintain	76.5	55.8	
Decrease	11.2	13.0	
Mean Support Score	(6) 2.01	(5) 2.18	*
Food Stamps			
Increase	15.7	24.6	
Maintain	59.4	51.0	
Decrease	24.9	24.4	
Mean Support Score	(7) 1.91	(7) 2.00	

[a] Two asterisks represent a difference between support scores of Representatives and the public of $p < .01$; one asterisk, $p < .05$.

[b] The mean scores are based on a scale from 1 (decrease) to 2 (maintain) to 3 (increase). The number in parentheses in front of the means are the rank order of the means from highest to lowest so the reader can more easily compare the ordering differences of the two groups.

groups as well—rich and poor, black and white, Democrats and Republicans, men and women—high levels of support exist in favor of Social Security and a consensus exists that society benefits from having the program.

The Views of Congressional Representatives

Levels of Support

Members of Congress support Social Security solidly; 97 percent favor increasing or maintaining benefits after taking into account cost-of-living increases, a level of support similar to that of the public (Table 6). The

Table 7
Support for Seven Social Welfare Programs
by Party of Representatives

| | Representatives at Large | | Social Welfare Committee Leaders | |
	Democrats Percent	Republicans Percent	Democrats Percent	Republicans Percent
Medicaid				
Increase	51.9	27.8	83.3	20.0
Maintain	48.1	59.3	16.7	80.0
Decrease	—	13.0	—	—
Mean[a]	2.52	2.15* [b]	2.83	2.20
AFDC				
Increase	31.6	34.2	58.3	20.0
Maintain	68.4	45.4	41.7	70.0
Decrease	—	19.4	—	—
Means Tested	—	0.9	—	10.0
Mean	2.32	2.15*	2.58	2.22
Medicare				
Increase	41.1	20.4	58.3	10.0
Maintain	54.2	57.4	41.7	60.0
Decrease	4.7	19.4	—	—
Means Tested	—	2.8	—	30.0
Mean	2.36	2.01*	2.58	2.14
SSI				
Increase	36.4	6.5	58.3	—
Maintain	63.6	74.1	41.7	100.0
Decrease	—	19.4	—	—
Mean	2.36	1.87***	2.58	2.00

proportion of Representatives favoring increases in Social Security benefits is much smaller than that of the general public, 12 percent of Congress versus 57 percent of the public. Two other differences are clear from the table: First, in contrast to the public, a majority of the Representatives favor increased benefits for *no* program. Second, the largest and most significant difference between the public and the Representatives is in support for programs that mainly serve the elderly. For Medicare, Social Security, and SSI, Representatives are significantly less likely to support increased benefits than are members of the general public.

Table 7 (cont.)
Support for Seven Social Welfare Programs
by Party of Representatives

	Representatives at Large		Social Welfare Committee Leaders	
	Democrats Percent	Republicans Percent	Democrats Percent	Republicans Percent
Social Security				
Increase	10.9	13.0	25.0	—
Maintain	89.1	80.6	75.0	100.0
Decrease	—	—	—	—
Means Tested	—	6.5	—	—
Mean	2.11	2.14	2.25	2.00
Unempl. Comp.				
Increase	16.6	6.5	41.7	—
Maintain	78.3	74.1	50.0	100.0
Decrease	5.2	19.4	8.3	—
Mean	2.11	1.87	2.33	2.00
Food Stamps				
Increase	21.7	7.4	50.0	10.0
Maintain	64.1	52.8	50.0	80.0
Decrease	14.1	39.8	—	10.0
Mean	2.08	1.68*	2.50	2.00

[a] The means are based on a 3 point scale from 1 (when decrease was response) to 2 (when maintain was response) to 3 (when increase was response).

[b] One asterisk indicates a difference between the support scores of Democrats and Republicans of $p < .05$; two asterisks, $p < .01$; and three asterisks, $p < .001$.

How do the privately expressed views of Representatives compare to their public actions in regard to Social Security? The most relevant indicator is the vote made in the preceding year on an amendment offered by Representative Marvin Leath (D, Texas) to the first budget resolution for fiscal year 1986 to eliminate COLAs for Social Security in order to produce additional deficit reduction. Of the anticipated savings, 20 percent would be added to programs that aid the poor elderly. Eighty-seven percent of the Representatives voted against this amendment, thus voting the same way they answered the survey question—that is, against any cuts in benefits.

Factors Related to Support

Democrats are reputed to support social welfare programs more than Republicans. The data in Table 7 confirm this view for all social welfare programs except Social Security. It receives similar levels of support from both Republicans and Democrats. The findings are similar for both leaders of committees having jurisdiction over social welfare policy issues and rank-and-file Representatives. That is, Democratic committee chairpersons are more supportive of most social welfare programs than are Republican ranking committee members. Again, the exception is Social Security, where the differences in support are trivial. What explains the support accorded to Social Security by Representatives and the similarity in support for Social Security between Republicans and Democrats?

Underneath the apparent support from Representatives are two quite different belief structures. One group of Representatives has highly favorable attitudes toward Social Security and wants to see it continue in its current form. I call this group the Committed Supporters. The second group has serious reservations about Social Security and would like to see the system altered, but supports the current system believing it is the only "safe" thing to do politically. I call this group the Reluctant Supporters.

Committed Supporters represent about 60 percent of the sample. The reasons for this group's support fall into two major categories, the explanation that people deserve their benefits because they have paid their taxes (as one member expressed it, "It's a program that we have established as a matter of right") and the explanation that it is a successful program (according to one, "the most successful and important of all the social programs"). Several legislators explicated their definition of success by pointing out that Social Security has helped to reduce poverty among the elderly. According to one midwestern Republican: "Social Security has been the most successful program that we've ever devised in terms of lifting people out of poverty. It's the one program you can point to and say absolutely we have succeeded in ending poverty in a certain class of people and that is the elderly. . . . 'Old' used to equate with 'poor,' and it doesn't anymore." Others added that it is now actuarially sound and Congress should keep "hands off" a program that is financially secure and working well.

Reluctant Supporters comprise about 40 percent of members. Their concerns fall into three categories. First, some are concerned about long-term implications of an aging society on Social Security—that is, more people are living longer and thus will need Social Security benefits for longer. They especially worry about the huge cohort of the baby boom generation, who will begin retiring in 2010. As one member said, "The system will bankrupt itself because all the post-World War II babies will come of age for Social Security at one time."

Second, some are concerned that people with high retirement incomes from other sources get Social Security they do not need. For example, one member quoted his father as saying, "I don't understand why I'm getting $1100 a month in Social Security benefits which I really don't need, and I can see neighbors who are struggling." Another said, "We have too many Americans living at or below the poverty level and not getting enough [benefits], and many who are practically wealthy and still receive Social Security. What I support is a means test. Our country is not ready for it at this time, but over time I think we are going to be driven to it. And one of the reasons why we are is the resentment of young Americans in footing the bill for wealthy Americans who, in their minds anyway, don't need it."

Third, and related to the latter part of the above comment, Reluctant Supporters are concerned about what they perceive to be the growing alienation among young adults and their increasing resentment about the burden of the employment tax. Two members, the first a Democrat and the second a Republican, expressed it this way:

> My children, my daughters who are between 23 and 33, have no faith at all that Social Security will be there for them. . . . And the young people say, 'Why should I be worried about my contribution to Social Security to pay recipients who are senior and improve their benefits when the program won't be there for me?' So you've got a kind of head-on collision here, and I hate to see this, you've got society pressure groups being created—senior citizens protecting their lot, junior citizens protecting what their lot is.

> I can see that it is going to get so bad that we are going to have an age split. Revolution, if you would. Maybe that's a little too strong a word, but the younger people are getting more and more fed up with paying such high rates. The young people are, on an increasing scale, becoming more and more alarmed about how much they are paying into the system, and becoming less and less accepting of the fact that there will be anything for them. Getting downright cynical. They are paying in all this and they know that the system will never be there when they get ready to retire.

Underlying these beliefs is worry about the deficit. For example, according to one Representative: "Everything you ask me is going to be colored by the fact that we have a budget deficit and that we are struggling to try and get a handle on that. And I envision some very hard economic times over the next few years. . . ."

Despite their concerns, the support for Social Security among Reluctant Supporters is similar to that of the Committed Supporters. Those Representatives who support Social Security while harboring doubts about it do so, they say, because they hear more from their constituents about Social Security than about any other social issue. Most of the public is supportive and the Representatives know it. As one member of Congress put it, "The Social Security program has been safe for a long time. It isn't about to collapse. That's about the last thing Congress would let collapse. They would wipe out national defense before they did that. I hate to say it, but I think they would." According to two others: "It's the mother lode; it's the Holy Grail around here. Nobody touches a hair on the head of Social Security." "When you talk Social Security, that's motherhood, that's apple pie."

Because Social Security is very popular and as a result of the policymaking process in regard to Social Security in the last few years, Reluctant Supporters hesitate to express their concerns about Social Security and to suggest any changes. For example, a Democrat from the South said: "For the Congress, [Social Security] is politically too hot to address. . . . The Republicans were burned severely in '82 with the way the Democrats demagogued Social Security. So, consequently, you end up with a standoff. Nobody wants to address those issues that are so politically volatile." A Republican from the West put it this way, "People are coming around and realizing that something has to be done. . . .but politically Social Security is just dynamite." A midwestern Republican commented, "[Social Security] is a political fact of life. . . . We are just virtually landlocked into maintenance. Politically, we have very little choice other than to maintain the program as it is."

Conclusion

Despite ten years of gloomy pronouncements about the viability of Social Security and about the public's willingness to continue supporting the Social Security system, members of the public continue to be extremely supportive of the program, not only in their attitudes but also in their professed willingness to take action. Those who are satisfied far outnumber the few people who are dissatisfied about paying Social Security taxes. Moreover, contrary to what some commentators claim, young adults strongly support Social Security and are just as willing to pay higher taxes to avoid cutbacks in benefits as other age groups.

Members of the House of Representatives also support Social Security. An overwhelming majority favors either maintaining or increasing benefits. In this respect, the opinions of the public and of Representatives converge. Currently, no "crisis" of support exists among members of the general public or of the House of Representatives.

In two other respects, however, the opinions of Representatives and the public diverge. First, the public is more likely to support an increase in benefits than are Representatives, perhaps because members of Congress are extremely concerned about the deficit and feel strong pressure not to increase spending, particularly for a program that is already indexed to the cost of living. Furthermore, members of Congress may be better informed than the public about costs. Representatives discussed the huge cost of the program and the impact of any increase in benefits on overall cost. Further, many believe that the fairly recent passage of the 1983 Social Security Amendments "fixed" Social Security for at least the immediate future and that the elderly, in general, do not need any increased assistance over and above COLA adjustments. In a part of the survey not reported here, members of the public and of Congress ranked which groups they thought should be given top priority for additional government assistance, food assistance, education-type services, and coverage against catastrophic illness.[32] Members of Congress were more likely than the public to give top priority to poor children, and less likely to give top priority to the elderly. Representatives pointed to growing rates of poverty among families with children and declining rates of poverty among the elderly. The public, in contrast, reported that they believe the elderly are needy and have few alternative sources of income. The different perspectives of Congress and the public on increasing Social Security benefits are reflected in these differences in their rankings.

The second and related way in which the opinions of congressional Representatives and the public diverge is in the belief structures that underlie their support decisions. This conclusion is tentative because Representatives did not answer exactly the same questions about their beliefs as did members of the public. For the public, two beliefs predict support for Social Security—the belief that all of society benefits because we have the Social Security program and the belief that many elderly have no sources of income other than Social Security. The beliefs of Representatives are less easily summarized. Some have few concerns about Social Security and are truly supportive of maintaining the system as it is, adjusting current benefits for inflation. They are the Committed Supporters. Others are superficially supportive in their voting and in comments to their constituents but actually do not want to maintain benefits as they are. These are the Reluctant Supporters.

Despite concern about the economic or political consequences of maintaining benefits, none of the Reluctant Supporters said they wanted to see

---

[32] Fay Lomax Cook, Edith J. Barrett, Susan J. Popkin, Ernesto A. Constantino, and Julie E. Kaufman, op. cit.

benefits reduced and only a handful voted to freeze COLAs. The reason is simple—the fear of public opinion. In other words, the reaction they anticipate from the public prevents them from seriously suggesting any alteration in Social Security that would entail reduction of benefits for the elderly. This is a classic use of what Kent Weaver has called "the politics of blame avoidance".[33] According to Weaver, ". . . .when push comes to shove, most officeholders seek above all not to maximize the credit they receive but to minimize blame. In formal terms, they are not credit-claiming maximizers but blame minimizers and credit-claiming and good policy satisfiers".[34]

Two interpretations of these findings are possible. One is that they should cause Social Security supporters concern. The House of Representatives is supportive on the surface but divided underneath. If some members of Congress have serious reservations about Social Security and do not re-open discussion about future directions only out of fear because Social Security is a politically volatile issue and they might get "burned," these results suggest that important issues are being muffled out of a desire by elected officials to avoid controversy and win re-election. Moreover, trouble for Social Security may lurk in the future, because divisiveness lies beneath the surface, waiting for the opportunity to erupt.

The second interpretation is that these findings should encourage both proponents of Social Security and democratic theorists. The public is supportive. Members of Congress know it and adjust their actions accordingly. Such adjustments correspond to some theories about democracy in which public opinion is—or is supposed to be—the great force behind the actions of government. According to this view, since support for Social Security is high among both the public and Congress, no problem exists for Social Security for the foreseeable future.

My conclusion lies somewhere in between the two. The support accorded to Social Security by both the public and Congress makes it secure for the immediate future, but not necessarily in the long run. We do not know what the impact on public support would be if the public should come to realize that although some Social Security recipients really need the income and have no alternative income sources, others do not have such a great need. As members of the public come to understand that some elderly have other sources of income—IRAs, stocks, bonds, and savings

[33] R. Kent Weaver, "The Politics of Blame Avoidance," *Journal of Public Policy*, Vol. 6, 1986, pp. 371–98.

[34] Ibid.

accounts—we do not know to what extent public support will shift. Re-search shows that most presentations of the elderly in the mass media, to date, have conformed either to what Binstock[35] has labelled the "compas-sionate stereotype of aging"—a view that shows the elderly to be financially needy and physically incapacitated—or to "the positive stereotype of aging"—a view that all elderly are economically and physically well-off. Relatively few media presentations have shown a complex and textured portrayal of the many sides of aging and the heterogenity of the aged.[36]

Currently, support for Social Security appears to rest to a large extent on the public's perception that society as a whole benefits because of Social Security and to a much smaller extent on the public's perceptions that Social Security recipients have no sources of income other than Social Security. If media portrayals shift to portray a stereotype of economic well-being among the elderly, then support for Social Security could decline. For the present, however, public support continues to be solid and strong. Support among a majority of U.S. Representatives appears to be solid and strong as well, although a significant minority expresses serious concerns.

[35] R.H. Binstock, "The Aged as Scapegoats," *The Gerontologist*, 1983, pp. 136–43.

[36] Bruce Jacobs, "Facts, Stereotypes, and Politics: Decisions on Programs for the Elderly," Paper presented at the Annual Meeting of the American Political Science Association, Chicago, IL, 1983 and "Seeking the Middle: Improving Public Discussion About Targeting Benefits for the Elderly," Report to the Ford Foundation, 1987.

Appendix Table 1
Demographic Characteristics of the Public Sample

	Public Sample N = 1209 (%)	Public Subsample[a] N = 495 (%)	United States Population[b] (%)
Age			
18–34	38.9	40.2	40.5
35–54	33.0	30.8	30.5
55–64	13.1	14.0	12.8
65 +	15.2	15.0	16.1
Gender			
Male	42.8	42.8	47.7
Female	57.2	57.2	52.3
Race			
White	86.1	85.8	86.3
Black	9.2	9.9	10.9
Other	4.6	4.2	2.8
Income			
Under $5,000	4.4	3.8	7.4
$5,000–9,999	9.7	8.3	11.6
$10,000–19,999	22.3	24.9	21.4
$20,000–34,999	27.0	27.2	26.2
$35,000–49,999	18.2	18.5	16.5
$50,000 +	18.4	17.2	16.8

[a] A subsample of the public was interviewed in greater depth about Social Security, as explained in the text.

[b] Source: Current Population Reports, Consumer Income, Series P-60, N-151, 1987. *Money Income of Households, Families, and Persons in the United States, 1986.* Income data are household income.

Appendix Table 2
Comparison of Characteristics of the Congressional Random Sample with Actual Membership of the House of Representatives

	Random Sample Weighted (N = 58)	Actual Membership (N = 435)
Party		
Republican	41.3	41.8
Democrat	58.6	58.1
Region		
East	23.4	23.9
Midwest	30.0	26.0
West	16.2	19.5
South	30.4	30.6
Education		
College Degree or Less	35.7	32.7
M.A./Ph.D.	10.0	24.1
Law Degree	54.3	43.7
Mean Age	50.1	49.7
Percent Minority		
Black	5.7	4.6
Hispanic	.6	2.8
Mean Years in Congress (Tenure)	8.25	8.38
Ratings of Votes by Organizations		
Children's Defense Fund (1985)	54.4	56.3
National Council of Senior Citizens (1985)	61.4	62.1
Americans for Democratic Action (1983 and 1984)	51.8	49.1
Americans for Constitutional Action (1983 and 1984)	45.1	46.7
National Journal—Social Issues (1985)	50.0	50.0
National Journal—Economic Issues (1985)	46.4	50.0
National Journal—Foreign Issues	48.5	50.0

DISCUSSION
Hugh Heclo*

FAY COOK'S PAPER OFFERS AN INFORMATIVE SNAPSHOT of where we are today with regard to public opinion and congressional support for the Social Security system. It is a picture that reveals broad public backing for the social insurance system. It is a picture showing a strong desire in Congress to stand pat with what we have—along with a significant shadow of concern about the viability of the Social Security system and few "profiles in courage" when it comes to giving public voice to these concerns.

Frankly, I am surprised that as many as 40 percent of members of Congress were willing to express their private worries to an interviewer on such a politically sensitive subject. Be that as it may, this research report yields absolute certainty on at least one point: members of Congress of every political persuasion are unanimous in refusing to say anything in public that could even remotely be considered as controversial regarding Social Security.

This demure posture among so many members of Congress is certainly understandable in a short-term political sense. But I think it is a weakness, not a strength, of the Social Security system when policymakers hide their worries and thus repress real public debate. The result is that there is no chance for corrective learning to occur through the open democratic process.

Fay Cook's still-life portrait of where we are today needs, I believe, to be supplemented with a view of tendencies that are at work shaping the future politics of Social Security. At least three signs of trouble are visible on the horizon.

First is the problem of the disappearing windfall. Social Security has

---

* Robinson Professsor of Public Affairs, George Mason University.

historically offered its participants an extremely large package of benefits in return for modest payroll tax contributions. This is the natural result of being in on the early stages of a pay-as-you-go public pension system; older workers passing into retirement have not had to contribute as long for their pension benefits as will those coming after them who have spent their entire lives in the system. Let me be clear. I am not saying Social Security will be a "bad deal" for workers in the years ahead. I am saying it will not represent the bonanza for retirees that it has in past decades. In a sense, the high rates of return Social Security offered allowed it to achieve popularity on the cheap. That is no longer possible in today's fully matured program. Higher-income single earners, in particular, are having to pay more for what they get of out the system.

A second sign of trouble to come is the strong possibility of higher payroll taxes in the future. Most observers now agree that Medicare hospital insurance faces major deficits, starting in the late 1990s and growing steadily larger in the next century. Higher taxes and/or benefit cuts will be required and the prospect of higher payroll taxes is especially strong if we hope to maintain a running actuarial balance in the years ahead. Again, I should not want to be misunderstood as painting an entirely negative picture. Over the past four decades huge payroll tax increases have occurred and proven politically tolerable. The point is that still higher deductions from take-home pay are going to be one more strain on the future politics of our social insurance system. They will have to be managed politically and absorbed by Americans most of whom are already paying more in payroll taxes than in income tax.

Thirdly, the elderly are no longer needier on average than other age groups. In the long history of social insurance, widely prevailing beliefs about the elderly as needy have undergirded political support for public pensions. Contemporary conditions are slowly but surely eating away at the ancient assumption equating age with deprivation. Indeed the elderly lobby itself is at pains to attack such age stereotyping and is helping persuade the public to see older persons as active, healthy, and productive citizens. Of course public policies, particularly Social Security, have been an important force in helping change the facts about elderly persons' well-being. At the same time, government policies have now also encouraged retirement saving, especially by the more affluent. These policies include tax deferral on income deposited in Individual Retirement Accounts, Keogh and other salary deferment schemes, and private pensions for workers fortunate enough to be in covered jobs. Economic inequality remains greater among the elderly than among the working-age population, and such inequality can be expected to persist and grow even further. The gap is likely to increase between those elderly who managed to get in on escalating housing prices and those who kept renting,[1] between those who landed the good jobs with stable earnings, generous fringe benefits, and tax-subsidized savings and those who did not.

In other words, there are good reasons for thinking there may be troubles on the horizon that could make Social Security less politically secure than it appears today. The reasons can be summarized in some straightforward questions that will, I predict, become increasingly prominent in our public conversation: Why are we paying higher taxes to support people who don't need it? Why are we transferring resources from the young regardless of ability to pay to the elderly regardless of need?

Unless we proceed carefully, those seemingly innocent questions pose great political challenges for our nation's social insurance system. The more we countenance a scaling-back and taxation of benefits to better-off people with private resources, the more we undermine the effective political constituency for an all-embracing Social Security program.

Of course no one (apart from some economists) sits down to calculate future returns on his or her payroll taxes. Everything, politically speaking, depends on underlying public perceptions and ways of understanding what is fair. Into this situation I have described comes lumbering the growing Social Security "surplus" of the 1990s (which of course is more accurately labeled as a reserve against future obligations). This multi-billion-dollar time-bomb might be called the amazing little secret of social policy in the 1980s. Through the 1983 Social Security amendments, Congress ordained that today's workers should not only pay for today's retirees but also contribute to a reserve fund that will help pay the bill for their own pensions in the future.

Creation of this fund is amazing because it seems quite at odds with the presumed tenor of the 1980s. How is it that we so prudently organized our affairs to relieve burdens on the next generation of taxpayers in the midst of the 1980s' me-first ethos of living for the moment? The answer is that the reserve fund is something that happened as a by-product of other decisions and with a minimum of informed public consent. I think it is fair to say that when it comes to this fund there simply is no public opinion. Ordinary people have never known enough about it to be able to form an opinion on the subject. The 1983 Social Security reforms were typical of much that goes on in Washington: policy-makers managed to fix a problem without creating a nationally understood policy. In short: smart politics, bad statecraft.

---

[1] John L. Palmer, "Financing Health Care and Retirement for the Aged." In Isabel V. Sawhill (ed.), *Challenge to Leadership*, The Urban Institute, 1988, p. 187.

What we are asking of our working-age population in the years ahead are not inhuman sacrifices but a certain degree of political understanding and forbearance. In a context of growing opportunities for some to organize private security packages, we are asking a good deal of forbearance when it comes to the "unearned" benefits of recent retirees and the dubious need of at least some elderly. We are asking for forbearance when it comes to a growing reserve fund and higher payroll taxes in a program that offers a poorer deal for younger, more affluent cohorts of the working population. In this regard it is interesting to observe in Fay Cook's paper the relatively lower level of support for Social Security that already exists today among higher-income whites.

My conclusion is that we are probably headed toward more political trouble than the current wisdom about Social Security's popularity allows. What I foresee is not a sudden convulsion but more of a slow-motion crisis as we leave the 1980s and such trends accumulate as the disappearing windfall, private provisions, distinctions among the elderly, worsening Medicare finances, higher payroll taxes, and poorly understood reserves. The simple historical fact is that Americans have never been able to accrue a substantial surplus in Social Security without spending it on some combination of higher pensions, new types of benefits, and/or lower taxes. That will in all likelihood happen in this case. The real question is not whether but how the reserve fund will be spent in the 1990s.

At a certain stage some political entrepreneur will, I hope, see that an important opportunity exists to win votes and incidentally do some good for the country. Solidarity has never been a particularly strong suit in American social policy. When invoked it has typically been seen to apply toward supporting the elderly. A strong case can be made, however, that there is another kind of generational solidarity, a debt mature Americans owe to the youngest generation, which is to say, the future. Using at least part of the Social Security reserve fund for investing in children is something that can be publicly understood and politically sold. The reserve fund makes sense as a way of providing for the future only if it helps raise productivity and economic growth over what it would have otherwise been. Indeed, productivity assumptions overpower any demographic changes, when it comes to forecasting our ability to pay for an aging population. Studies of economic growth are quite clear on the fact that enlarging the size of the pie depends primarily, not on national saving, but on technological advances and the education and skills of the work force. Today children at risk of failure are the fastest-growing segment of the school population. We know how to bring healthy babies into the world, but too often we do not do it. We know the importance of the first years of life and the payoff from early childhood development programs, but we leave disadvantages to accumulate among the most vulnerable children. We spend huge amounts to clean up the social wreckage among young adults that could have been prevented earlier by prudent investments in children.

Someday perhaps someone more politically adept than I will make the connection between social insurance and investment in the coming generation. When that occurs we will have done both ourselves and our children a favor.

DISCUSSION
Karlyn Keene*

A S AN EDITOR OF A MAGAZINE THAT HAS FOCUSED ON
survey data for more than a decade, I have been looking at public
opinion polls on Social Security for a long time.
As you know, we as a society are accumulating enormous quantities of
data that too often contribute to confusion rather than clarity in a complex
policy environment. It is useful, then, to have a survey that adds to our
understanding, and I believe that Fay Cook's survey does that. It also has
the advantage of breaking some new ground by comparing responses of
members of Congress and the public to identical questions.

This survey confirms a picture that we have been getting from Social
Security data for several decades. Support is high. It crosses generational
lines, in part because the public believes the program benefits society and
that those who receive it deserve the help. The ends the public wants to
achieve with Social Security are not in doubt.

I have three specific reservations about the survey, and then I would like
to offer some general comments about public opinion in this area.

Cook reported that support for Social Security is higher than support for
six other governmental programs she examined. I do not doubt that support for Social Security is high and abiding, but I would be more satisfied
with the comparative responses if we knew what levels of information the
public had about the other programs. It is essential to ascertain basic levels
of knowledge before making these kinds of comparisons.

I also have reservations about questions on public willingness to have
taxes raised in areas that are under discussion in Washington these days. I
am not at all surprised that Americans say they are willing to pay extra

---

* Managing Editor, *Public Opinion*.

money for Social Security, but does looking at that question in isolation really tell policymakers very much?

In a survey for *Times Mirror* last year, the Gallup organization asked Americans about twelve different areas. The question was framed in a useful way. In a four-part question, Americans were asked whether an area was not much of a problem, whether it was a problem but one that required no government action, whether the area was a problem that required government action only if no new taxes were needed, and finally, was the problem such that it required government action even if new taxes were necessary.

In only three of twelve areas did majorities say that they felt the problem was serious enough that new taxes might be required. Significantly, one of those three areas was to provide a decent standard of living for the elderly. But in other areas, such as ensuring that every American has a place to sleep and food to eat, or providing a job for everyone who wants one, only bare pluralities suggested that the problem was serious enough that new taxes would be required to address it.

It is important to put questions about raising taxes in perspective.

In another survey done recently by The Public Agenda Foundation, six social programs were examined, including Headstart, WIC, and basic health insurance for the working poor. Four in ten Americans said that they would be willing to pay $25 a year to have these programs expanded, but only a minority were willing to pay more than $25 a year for any of them, even the most popular of the programs, long-term care for the elderly.

If we look at the messages that voters were sending in the 1988 election, we find again a mixed message on the issue of taxes. When NBC asked voters whether or not the deficit was serious enough to have our taxes raised, a substantial plurality (45 percent) said that the deficit was not serious enough to have our taxes raised. When CBS and *The New York Times* went back to talk to voters after the election, about 66 percent of Americans suggested that George Bush would probably raise taxes but 64 percent of Americans said that he should not raise them.

We need to be very careful in looking at taxing-and-spending questions in isolation.

A third point is the cleavage that Cook showed between the congressional sample and the general-public sample on maintaining or increasing benefits. That may be the by-product of the different levels of information the two groups have and little more than that.

It is important to focus on what Americans are really telling us in these surveys. Serious mischief is done when politicians assume that the public is providing specific guidance on issues like family leave, child care, or mandated health benefits. The public knows what ends it wants served in the case of Social Security, but there is little evidence that the public is providing us specific guidance on the means that should be used to accomplish these ends in a complex policy environment.

Survey questions in this area seem to sort out in different ways. We have questions where people give us answers, but we know that they have very little specific interest and very low levels of information. We have other questions where people have fully formed opinions with a very high level of awareness. This is true about Social Security, or, more precisely, the ends that the programs should serve.

Then a whole group of questions falls somewhere in between. Public opinion is not fully formed, but the underlying value is so strong that any attempt to tinker with it is politically perilous; not impossible, but politically difficult.

Looking ahead to the consideration of Social Security reforms, to the alterations that might be made in the system, I would argue that they generally fall into this third category. When Ronald Reagan made a statement in the spring of 1981 about Social Security and the Senate unanimously rebuffed him, he was seen, I believe, as trifling with the underlying value: a strong commitment to the Social Security system.

Public opinion can act as a damper on leadership when it is not properly understood. Issues dealing with reforms of or alterations to the Social Security system fall into this third category, where public opinion is not fully formed and where there is substantial room for bold legislators to maneuver.

I would add one final observation. Cook began her paper by discussing the three different ways that Social Security had been described in terms of the crisis rhetoric. As someone who has been around Washington for nearly 20 years now, it seems to me that we lurch from one crisis to the next, and it is not just in the area of Social Security. If you read the book review section of *The New York Times* a few weeks ago, you would have found that there is a crisis of the modern American novel. "Crisis" is the standard rhetoric with which we describe problems of our society.

A real challenge for policymakers is to tone down the crisis rhetoric. Perhaps then we will be able to restore young people's confidence in the system, or at least in our ability to address its problems.

DISCUSSION

Norman Ornstein*

W E ARE FOCUSING ON PUBLIC OPINION IN A CONFER-
ence on Social Security and the Budget to try to understand the
political context that policymakers face as they deal with the
budget. It is quite clear, as Fay Cook's research shows and as Karlyn Keene
suggested (and contrary to at least some of the conventional wisdom), that
the overwhelming mass of public opinion supports Social Security and
does so intensely.

I helped design some of the *Times Mirror* questions to which Karlyn
Keene referred. We tried to get much more directly at trade-offs that are
rarely examined in public opinion questions. We wanted to find out not just
whether people supported programs but where they would spend money to
back that support. We found few areas where they would. Clearly, the
willingness to pay higher taxes for a particular program underscores where
support for government programs is intense.

The fact that supporting and protecting the standard of living of the
elderly was one of only three out of twelve different policy areas where the
public is prepared to spend more, does tell us something about the level of
intensity. These public opinion data tell us something more, I think. We
should look a bit more deeply at why we see this support for Social Security.
Let me throw out a couple of hypotheses.

First, it is quite clear, as Fay Cook's research and others before have
suggested, that young people support Social Security at least as strongly as
the elderly. Why? Part of the explanation is self-interest. Many younger
people view the alternative as having to support their parents or grand-
parents. For many younger people, particularly women, this is not a question of "us versus them." Women especially understand that a strong Social

---

*Resident Scholar, American Enterprise Institute.

Security program, by protecting the standard of living of the elderly, enables the elderly to be independent. Jeopardizing Social Security puts not only the elderly but also the young at risk directly. The strong support for Social Security reflects two broader underlying aspects of Social Security. Americans see value received through this program in return for what they pay. The benefits are not seen in abstract terms. Of course, the reality, that until now beneficiaries have put in far, far less than they got back in return, has something to do with the program's appeal. The intense reaction of many elderly people who are heavily taxed by the catastrophic health insurance plan that was passed last year underscores this point. Because many elderly people believe that they are going to have to pay in a whole lot more directly and get very little back, we hear tremendous rumblings, especially from the better-off elderly who have had their own supplemental health insurance that in many instances was broader and better than what they will get with the catastrophic health plan. This different public reaction is going to put additional pressure on policymakers down the road.

A second aspect is the fundamental American value of fairness. People see the Social Security system as, by and large, fair because you put something in and you get something back. It is not as if I am putting in the money and somebody else is getting benefits that I will never recover. I must say that I saw this in a very direct and tangible way, as many others of you have, when the issue of unfairness came up a couple of years ago; I inadvertently mentioned the notch babies on MacNeil/Lehrer. I got flooded with mail that reflected the widely held view that Social Security treats unfairly one group of the elderly.

In the future, as Hugh Heclo noted, more people may begin to see the system as unfair, as people become aware of the fact that the Social Security tax is the single largest tax burden that they bear. That is true now for most Americans, and it will become true for even more over the next several years. As that happens, reactions may change and may lead, among other things, to reform of the Social Security tax to make it less regressive.

Social Security is also part of the current budget debate. First, in deciding how to cut the deficit, we must consider to what extent we want to reduce expenditures. And that raises the question of whether to pare back the cost-of-living adjustments. Second, even if we do nothing to cut benefits, we must decide what to do with the growing reserves. In particular, is it prudent or desirable to use those surpluses to mask the deficit on other government programs? Interesting discussions and political ramifications are going to flow from the strong public opinion that is out there about Social Security.

Policy may well move away from these two questions directly and more toward an increase in taxation of benefits. If you tax benefits, as opposed to cutting back on expenditures, and then put the proceeds into the general revenue fund, you are not directly dipping into the reserves to pay for current deficits; benefit cuts may then be less necessary two or three decades hence to meet deficits that appear in the future. I think, as we become more sharply focused on those two issues, we are going to turn more in our policy discussions towards taxation of benefits.

And, particularly, as we move ahead, we are going to see a sharper difference between the haves and have-nots among the elderly. Whatever the political climate, I would not be surprised if we revisit Social Security in about five years to make the system fairer, both by taxing benefits more and by altering the payroll tax base. In my judgment, that would not be a bad direction in which to go.

PANEL ON FORMULATING A DEFICIT REDUCTION PACKAGE: WHAT IS THE ROLE OF SOCIAL SECURITY?

FIRST PRESENTATION

Robert M. Ball*

I N CONNECTION WITH SHORT-TERM BUDGET DECISIONS, there is no good reason at all to consider Social Security. This simple, straightforward assertion is true not only for current deficit reduction decisions, but for short-term budget decisions in general.

Social Security is a long-term program. People today are paying for benefits that they may not collect for up to half a century. To start messing around with this program because of non-Social Security problems in the general budget is a mistake and destructive of people's confidence in the program.

In 1983, things were different. A major problem within the Social Security system itself had to be fixed. The 1983 changes, which were for the most part quite marginal, won general support because they were entirely changes needed by Social Security.

We are not in that situation now. Social Security is in good shape and public support for the provisions as they are is strong. By and large, we just ought to leave Social Security alone.

This statement does not imply that well-off older people ought not to be part of solving the deficit problem. But Social Security is not the way. Average monthly benefits under Social Security for retired workers are $525. Yet Social Security is the major source of income for two-thirds of the older beneficiaries.

---

*Commissioner of Social Security, 1962 to 1973.

To make the well-off elderly—and, incidentally, the well-off non-elderly as well—be part of the solution, we ought to restore an additional income tax bracket or two above the 28 percent bracket. I, for one, am eager to pay more taxes. And I do not think I am alone. While the well-off ought to be paying more in taxes, cuts in Social Security generally or in the cost-of-living adjustment (COLA) affect mostly the wrong people.

Still, some changes are desirable because they make sense for Social Security and also contribute to deficit reduction. One such change would be to make coverage universal. Only one sizable group is now left out of Social Security: the 30 percent of state and local employees, about four million people, who have not been brought in under the voluntary provisions in present law.

It is particularly unfair to the rest of the population to excuse this group from Medicare contributions. Most state and local employees pick up Medicare coverage through employment other than their state and local jobs, or they are covered as dependents of those eligible for Medicare. By not paying for Medicare throughout their careers, as does everybody else, they end up with exactly the same package of benefits with fewer payments. That is clearly unfair, because other workers have to support benefits for this group. Covering this group would increase Medicare income about $9 billion over five years, which would help Medicare and reduce the budget deficit.

In the OASDI program, policy for state and local employees ought to be the same as that for federal employees: All new employees should be covered under Social Security with state and local plans modified as desired to build on top of Social Security like all other retirement systems. Over the next five years this change would increase Social Security income about $8 billion and help reduce the budget deficit by this amount.

On the other hand, it would be a mistake to change the Social Security COLA. Designing a retirement system to pay lower benefits to people as they grow older makes no sense, but that is exactly what happens if the program pays less than a full COLA. Whatever level of benefits is considered desirable when first paid ought to at least be kept up to date with purchasing power throughout retirement.

Another point to be kept in mind is that major permanent cuts in Social Security benefits are not likely to help the deficit over time because such cuts would trigger corresponding cuts in Social Security income. It is unlikely that people could be persuaded to pay higher Social Security contributions than would be necessary to pay for the reduced protection.

But supposing someone came to me and said, "O.K., we understand that you don't think it desirable to have Social Security involved in deficit reduction, but no sizable reduction package is politically viable without having Social Security involved. What would you do?"

If that were the issue presented, I would certainly say that the best case is for taxing more of the Social Security benefits of higher-income beneficiaries. The problem is that the burden would fall on the same group being asked to pay the income-related premium for the new catastrophic health plan. How soon and how often you should ask the same people to pay higher taxes is a real question.

But on the merits and taken alone, the case for taxing more of Social Security benefits is strong. Tax policy for Social Security should match that applied to all other retirement systems. The basic tax rule is that the recipient of a pension pays a tax on benefits that exceed his or her own contributions out of previously taxed income. If this rule were applied to the Social Security benefits of higher-income people, about 85 percent of Social Security benefits would be included in adjusted gross income instead of up to 50 percent of benefits.

There really is no good reason why Social Security was treated differently from other retirement benefits from the beginning. The complete exemption of benefits from taxation, which lasted until the 1983 Amendments, was an accidental result of the way the program was designed. Its authors feared back in 1935 that the Supreme Court might find a Federal program of social insurance requiring contributions and benefits based on those contributions to be unconstitutional. Consequently, the benefit provisions and the taxing provisions were kept in separate titles of the Social Security Act. No one doubted the power of Congress to levy taxes or to pay benefits, but some thought there was a problem in connecting the two; so the two functions were separated.

When the Treasury looked at the law after it was passed, it determined the benefits were a "gratuity" because they were not connected to the contributions paid in, and gratuities aren't taxable to the recipient. The exemption of Social Security benefits from taxation rested not on law, but on this rather dubious Treasury ruling. In any event, Congress subjected a portion of Social Security benefits to income tax in 1983, and the case for taxing more of the benefit is compelling. I have favored taxing Social Security benefits as other pensions are taxed for at least 25 years. I believe it strengthens the perception of the benefit as earned and is one more way of distinguishing Social Security from welfare and associating it with other payments growing out of work, such as wages and pensions. It is not a gratuity.

Some other changes in long-range financing arrangements are worth considering, although they are not directly associated with the present deficit crisis. Under current law, reserves will rise sharply, reach a peak around 2030, and be dissipated gradually in the succeeding two decades. Whether this is the best way to finance the system over the long term is highly questionable.

A big, one-time buildup of reserves and then their liquidation might make sense if we were dealing with a temporary jump in costs because of the large baby boom generation. But that is not the situation. If mortality rates continue to fall and fertility rates remain low, two reasonable assumptions, the rise in benefit costs is permanent, not temporary. The baby boom generation begins a new plateau of higher costs. The lower ratio of workers to beneficiaries that will occur when the baby boom generation retires will persist as mortality rates fall further and fertility stays low.

If we are going to build Social Security reserves, as called for by present law, we ought to maintain them. One way to do so is to schedule a tax rate increase around, say, 2030 of about 1 percentage point for employees and the same for employers. Reserves continue to increase under this plan, although less rapidly than benefit payments. At the end of the 75 years over which the estimates are made, the reserve equals about one or one and one-half times the next year's outgo, a reasonable contingency reserve. Social Security could then continue on a pay-as-you-go basis.

Or we might go to a pay-as-you-go system in the early 1990s when the fund will become adequate for a contingency reserve, a result that could be accomplished by moving some of the OASDI contribution rate to Medicare, which will be substantially underfunded early in the next century even on a pay-as-you-go basis. Pay-as-you-go for OASDI (with a substantial contingency reserve) is a workable alternative to building up a big earnings reserve, but there are disadvantages. For one thing, ultimate contribution rates would have to be somewhat higher than those under current law to make up for the lack of interest earnings on the reserves. More important, if a reserve build-up in Social Security results in a surplus or a lower deficit in the unified accounts of the government—that is, if the Social Security buildup does not just substitute for higher general taxes—then the reserves increase the national saving rate and contribute to a greater pool of goods and services in the future. The result of this would make it easier to pay future Social Security benefits. This benefit from trading less now for more later is not present under pay-as-you-go.

The current approach of building up a large reserve and then running it down came about more or less by accident. It is the result of policy decisions made for other reasons. One of the biggest issues in the early days of Social Security was whether or not to build a substantial reserve. The issue was never fully settled. Until 1972 the system operated more or less on a pay-as-you-go basis in practice and a sizable reserve basis in theory. The law always contained contribution rates, scheduled to take effect later, that would have built big reserves had they been allowed to go into effect. The actuarial evaluations of the program used these scheduled rate increases to show the system to be in long-range balance, but whenever the theory of reserve accumulation threatened to become reality the Congress postponed tax increases, and the projected buildup in reserves did not occur. Nevertheless, Social Security was always balanced in the long-range actuarial estimates by taking into account those scheduled increases. The real control on cost in Social Security has been the long-range cost estimates, not the short-term situation.

In 1972, on the advice of the 1971 Advisory Council, the Congress openly adopted a pay-as-you-go approach. At the same time, however, in order to make the system balance over the traditional seventy-five year period, the Congress enacted a rate increase to take effect in 2011 that preserved actuarial balance over the succeeding seventy-five years. The large rate increase scheduled for 2011 was an alternative to a series of small rate increases from 2011 on. Planners assumed that in 2011 the one-time rate increase would be changed to a pay-as-you-go schedule.

In 1977, Congress moved the 2011 rate increase up to 1990, to help meet an estimated deficit. Projections indicated that a sizable reserve would result. Then the 1983 Amendments moved part of the 1990 rate increase up to 1988 and also in various other ways increased projected reserve accumulation.

Allowing the new 1988 rate to go into effect shifted the system from pay-as-you-go to partial reserve funding. This outcome was not so much a deliberate decision to abandon pay-as-you-go financing as it was a decision to build back up to an adequate contingency reserve. Moreover, if any part of the rate schedule had been postponed, without additional tax increases in later years, the system would no longer have been in close actuarial balance. Furthermore, the rate increase was very convenient for Gramm-Rudman-Hollings purposes.

My conclusion is that Social Security works under either pay-as-you-go or partial reserve financing. Accumulating a partial reserve while moving toward balance in the non-Social Security budget has the advantage of increasing the saving rate in the United States, and I have a preference for this build-up of the reserve. But the question of whether or not to build a reserve is not primarily a Social Security issue. We can do Social Security either way. We should not treat reserve accumulation as the result of a thought-through proposal adopted by the National Commission on Social Security Reform. If that happened, it was when I was out of the room.

However the reserve issue is eventually settled, I think it important to get Social Security out of deficit reduction targets. Counting Social Security annual surpluses for deficit reduction purposes results in pressure to increase those surpluses by benefit cuts. I do not think Social Security can be taken out of the Gramm-Rudman-Hollings targets all at once, however. Doing so would put too much pressure on all the rest of the budget. I would propose that Social Security stay in the Gramm-Rudman-Hollings targets until 1993, the end point of the Gramm-Rudman-Hollings law, and that after that Social Security annual surpluses be gradually removed from the measurement of the deficit, say at a rate of 15 to 30 percent a year.

SECOND PRESENTATION

James Jones*

THE QUESTION THAT FACES THIS PANEL IS WHAT ROLE, IF any, Social Security should play in deficit reduction. I hold that every segment of our society must play some role in the deficit reduction process. Reducing the annual deficits and the accumulated national debt are so vital and urgent that nobody and no segment of our society, except those truly in the most desperate need, should be excused from participating in solving that problem. I say that for two reasons. First, if allowed to persist, this deficit will lower the standard of living for the next generation. They will have to pay their own obligations as well as the outstanding obligations that we have run up. I think this is a moral issue and it is unfair to the next generation.

Secondly, although the deficit, per se, is unlikely to cause a cataclysmic drop in the economy, the more that deficit grows and debt accumulates, the more we are unable to be the masters of our own destiny. As that debt grows, and particularly as it is owned in larger measure by foreign interests, our monetary policy, as well as our fiscal policy, has to pay more attention to foreign interests and less to our own domestic concerns. And I think this limits our sets of priorities.

In short, the deficit has to be dealt with, because if it is not, it will undermine economic growth and the premise of the stability of the Social Security trust fund.

In the fourteen years I was in Congress, I twice voted on major Social Security bills to "save Social Security." In 1977 we enacted a large tax increase to "save Social Security for the next seventy-five years." That promise was based on honest projections of economic growth that did not materialize. So by 1983, we were told that Social Security checks would not

---

* Chairman of the House Budget Committee, 1981 to 1984.

be in the mail in July 1983 if we didn't have another legislative bailout. We had to save it again. Now the trust fund is sound and the reserves are growing. But, again, as we look to the future, the system remains dependent on economic growth.

My argument is that the huge overall budget deficits threaten to undermine economic growth if we do not deal with them. Everybody has to play a part in doing so. Those who want to attack Social Security sometimes allege that retired people are not willing to participate. I say that is definitely wrong. I will give you two examples from the early 1980s when I was Chairman of the House Budget Committee. We predicted in 1981 that the supply-side economic program would indeed create these huge deficits, and my predictions were accurate. Because of the emerging debt and the economic impact on the future of Social Security, I introduced a couple of bills to get people to talking and thinking about ways to keep the trust fund solvent. These discussion bills would limit the cost-of-living adjustments. One of them would limit the COLAs to a formula of a CPI minus 2 percent. The other, in essence, would make the annual COLAs an ad hoc decision by Congress and the President.

I went to one of the major organizations representing retired Americans. I spoke to their national board of directors and was told before I spoke, "Don't mention your COLA limitation legislation because that will get everybody upset." I said, "Well, if the question comes up, I will take it head on and be honest about it."

A question came up, and I explained why I thought that it was important that this had to be under consideration. Not really to my surprise, but I think to the surprise of some of the staff of that organization, everybody on that board, except, I think, two people, expressed support for that or some similar concept, provided everybody else shared in the sacrifice to get this budget mess under control.

Again in 1985, some of the Republican leaders in the Senate offered legislation that would limit the growth of Social Security benefits. They worked closely with organizations representing retired Americans' and, again, the level of support among older Americans' groups was virtually unanimous so long as everybody else participated in the sacrifice and this was for the national good. As many of you recall, the rug was pulled out from under the Republican leadership by their own administration at the White House, and nothing came of the legislative effort.

But the point is this: I do not agree with those who say that older Americans want more than their fair share and that they are greedy or they will not participate. That is not true and I have had two specific experiences that permit me to say that they are as willing as any segment of our society to participate in what is good for our national economy.

Having said that, I guess we ought to look specifically at some ways in which Social Security can participate. First, I would not raid the Social Security reserves to finance new programs. Doing so would be a mistake, and it would just exacerbate the deficit reduction problem and postpone its solution.

Second, I would not use surpluses in Social Security trust funds surpluses to mask the general budget deficit. As you know, Social Security is in a hybrid accounting situation, for purposes of Gramm- Rudman, until the 1993 fiscal year. Until then, Social Security surpluses can be used to lower this unified budget deficit. After that, Social Security goes off budget. The temptation will be to keep postponing dealing with the Federal deficit as long as that Social Security trust fund can be used to reduce the general deficit. I would like to see Social Security removed from the unified budget before 1993, so that the Congress and the Administration would be forced to deal honestly with the growing general budget deficit.

Some things should be done. First of all, I think you have to analyze the trust fund, in its component parts. The Medicare portion of the trust fund is in trouble. It faces bankruptcy just after the turn of the century. Solutions must be found before that.

Several proposals should be considered, such as: requiring coverage for more segments of our population; reducing payments to the suppliers; increasing taxes in a pay-as-you-go effort, and adding to the progressivity of the tax on the health care benefits.

We have to give real attention to the progressivity of Social Security benefits in general. It has always amazed me that the same people who talk the loudest about the need for progressivity in our Federal tax-benefits structure say it is unfair to have progressivity for retired Americans. To me, that doesn't make any sense.

My parents lacked education and lived through the Depression. They badly needed Social Security. If I continue to be fortunate, I will not need it, and I should be taxed progressively more than those who need the benefits more. I favor extending what was done in the 1983 Social Security Act Amendments and lowering the threshold of taxation on previously untaxed Social Security benefits. That change ought to be part of the deficit reduction package.

We should explore ways to invest Social Security trust fund reserves in longer-term government securities, perhaps using some of the surpluses to buy out shorter-term, higher interest cost Federal debt. If we can buy down any of this short-term, high interest rate debt, we should save on annual debt service cost.

To keep the Social Security reserves from being used just to finance new programs, I think we should explore how to invest Social Security reserves in private securities, a course followed by some state pension programs that is currently not allowed by law. Strict limits would be necessary, but this capital ought to be put to use for economic growth.

We should also be trying to extend the useful productive lives of older Americans. That should be done by a system of incentives to get people to work longer and to train people to work better. By the mid 1990s, we are going to have a labor shortage yet we will have trained, productive older workers. If we can keep them active, it will help economic growth and take pressure off the need to make sacrifices to get this deficit under control.

THIRD PRESENTATION
Carol G. Cox*

L ET ME START WITH A QUESTION. DO THOSE OF YOU who think that Social Security should be exempt from any benefit reductions or changes in tax treatment because the trust fund is in surplus feel that way because of the way we finance the program, or because of the way you feel about the program?

Or, to put it another way, assume that we had a dedicated tax to pay for defense and that the defense trust fund were in surplus. Would you, therefore, argue that we should abjure any discussion of defense spending, relative to our other priorities?

The sheer size of the Social Security program makes it virtually impossible for me to imagine any deficit-reduction package that has any political support that does not do something with that program. Outlays on Social Security and Medicare today exceed outlays on defense. By the mid to late 1990s, the OASDI program alone is projected to be larger than our defense expenditures.

You may think that is perfectly appropriate. I must say to you that I do not believe, in the trite old phrase, that you can take the biggest programs in the budget off the table and come up with a saleable deficit reduction package, whether you are talking about defense, Social Security, or Medicare.

Some people say to me, " Social Security is self-funded." I have to tell you that self-funding is a myth. I have been all over the United States looking for self, and he doesn't exist. The fact of the matter is that the same taxpayers who pay Social Security taxes also pay all other Federal taxes.

You all know the change in the composition of Federal revenues since the early 1960s. Social insurance revenues equal about 4 percent more of

---

* President, Committee for a Responsible Federal Budget.

gross national product than they did in 1960. All other Federal revenues
have been cut by about 3 percent of gross national product since 1960.
Although total Federal revenues have increased by nearly 1 percent of GNP,
we have about 2.3 percent less of GNP than we had 28 years ago, or about
$115 billion a year in current prices, to pay for all of the non-social insurance
activities of government. Does anyone really think we can cut our government spending by those amounts, without cutting big programs like Social
Security? I do not think so.

I must say to you also that there are trade-offs between a commitment to
social insurance and a commitment to the most vulnerable in this society. I
have watched, in the 1980s, as we have cut programs that served the needs
of the most poor and the most vulnerable in this country because politically
they were more vulnerable than the recipients of social insurance programs
that serve a larger population and were, therefore, more popular.

I think the issues of progressivity that Jim Jones talked about are very
important, and I must report to you that, as we go around the country, we
find that people are more concerned with progressivity than you may think.
In the past year, we have done an Exercise in Hard Choices in eleven cities
with over 1,000 people, with several Members of Congress and one gover-
nor. We have sat down with groups of eight or ten people, old and young,
business and labor. We have watched them go through a deficit reduction
exercise, and I can report to you that people, as they look at Medicare and
Social Security, do not have the same commitment to the social insurance
concept that some of you may have. They want progressive ways to cut
those programs. They want to put those programs on the table. Even the
retired people in those audiences feel you have to do something in that part
of the budget if you are going to come up with a balanced package,
whatever that means.

They want to do things that bear less heavily on the poorer people and
more heavily on those who are better off. For that reason, I suspect, Mr.
Ball, most of the audiences do prefer taxing Social Security benefits to
cutting COLAs though on a short-term basis, I report to you, a majority
would do something to COLAs as well. Probably the most heartening thing
that we discovered in this exercise, as we went from city to city and place to
place, was that people seem to feel duty bound to put things on the table
that matter to them. In Sacramento, the huge majority of the groups voted
to raise excise taxes on beer and wine. Vic Fazio, Democratic Congressman
from California's 4th District, who was our co-host, said to the audience,
"Don't you know how dependent this economy is on wine?" One of the
women in the audience replied: "Vic, we like our wine, but we will pay for
it." We went to Arizona and cotton farmers said they would raise prices for
Federal reclamation water. For those of you who have never been in

western states like Arizona, that is a very significant thing for them to say. Throughout the Midwest, in Des Moines and Topeka and Omaha, audiences said, "Yes, we must cut agricultural price supports; we understand that will bear not only on our farmers but on the general economy of our areas, but we can't shift this burden off onto other people's shoulders."

The politics, if not the arithmetic, are such that every single item in the budget will be on the table, if and when we ever do what we must to deal with this deficit problem. It is unrealistic to think that we can insulate large programs, like Social Security or Medicare. Many of the people we encountered were sophisticated about Social Security and Medicare. That is not an accident. AARP helped pay for the exercises we did around the country.

They said things like: "Okay, if we increased taxes on Social Security, would we put the money in the trust fund or would we put it in general revenues?" Frankly, I think some would have liked an option to have cut Social Security benefits and cut Federal Insurance Contributions Act taxes but we didn't have that option in our exercise, so I can't tell you how broad the support for that would have been. I can tell you that many said: "Well, you could put it in the trust fund and use it to offset the general fund contribution to Part B of Medicare." That is a fairly high degree of sophistication, I grant you, but understand we had people from AARP in many of these groups, and they understand how those programs work. That approach could make a very significant contribution to reducing the overall deficit. The financing structure for Social Security is not sufficient justification for isolating it from any discussion of what we do vis-à-vis other priorities.

Perhaps the most dangerous aspect of Federal fiscal policy over the last several years is that it has limited our ability to deal with new needs and new priorities. Perhaps the most bizarre aspect of our recent decision-making processes is that we subject our new high-priority initiatives to a much tougher test than we apply to anything that has been on the books for five or ten or fifty years. A new catastrophic health insurance program has got to be deficit neutral. To pay for it we have to cut other programs or raise taxes.

To start initiatives for the homeless or anything else requires a way to pay for it. We don't subject programs that are on the books today to that kind of scrutiny. When we do, you will see pressure for spending reductions the likes of which you have not seen yet, even in the 1980s. When we propose to raise taxes or cut other programs to pay for what we want our government to do, and when we propose to raise revenues sufficiently to pay for what we are getting from government today, you will see real pressure for spending restraint.

You will see that pressure because you have never had a spending revolt in this country. We have had tax revolts and politicians remember them. Raising taxes is a painful activity for a politician. One of the most interesting aspects of the exercise we have done is that, as a group, politicians are more reluctant to raise taxes than any other identifiable constituency that has ever done the exercise.

It is fact, folks.

When you start saying, "Okay, put up or shut up," and, "If we can't cut spending, we are going to raise revenues, but we are going to balance the budget on a reasonable set of economic assumptions in the foreseeable future," you will see really serious pressure to cut spending, I fearlessly predict to you. I only hope that, when we do cut spending, we will do so as broadly as we can across the budget, the economy, and the nation. It continues to surprise me as a budgeteer that, after many years of incredibly high deficits, we could go into a room in the middle of the night, make the changes needed to put our fiscal house in order, not tell anybody what we had done—and nobody would notice.

The great surprise to me is that the changes that would solve the deficit problem are still relatively marginal. We are not talking about the politics of real sacrifice. We are talking about modest restraint. That is the best argument there is for doing what needs to be done now, because if we wait for another recession or what economists so aridly call some "exogeneous" event to force our hand, we could be looking at much more drastic remedies.

FOURTH PRESENTATION

Alan S. Blinder*

THE TOPIC OF THIS SESSION IS THE ROLE OF SOCIAL
Security in deficit reduction. When I was given that title many
months ago, I interpreted it as referring to the macroeconomic role.
That is the way I just naturally think about things; but it is apparently quite
different from everybody else's way of thinking. So let me first say that I
agree with everything said by the previous speakers and proceed to think
about the issue macroeconomically.

The first thing that comes to mind when I think about Social Security
and the budget is the quip Adlai Stevenson made regarding the peregrina-
tions of John Foster Dulles: Don't just do something, stand there. As you
know, if there are no changes in policy, Social Security will, through its own
annual surplus, help reduce the overall deficit. Whether we put the annual
Social Security surpluses into the Social Security trust fund or into the
general fund is immaterial. What matters is the overall balance of saving
and investment in the economy and what the government is doing to that
balance.

That is all obviously true. But I am afraid that many, many people—and I
am one of them, I must confess—have exaggerated the help we are going to
get from Social Security without any further changes in policy. Let me deal
separately with the short and long runs.

In the short run, by which I mean until the horizon of the Gramm-
Rudman-Hollings targets (which happens, by coincidence, to be the end of
the Bush Administration), the law mandates a reduction of the budget
deficit from the currently projected $155 billion in 1989 to zero by 1993—
including Social Security. By contrast, the Congressional Budget Office
baseline shows that, under current policies, including current Social Security policies, the deficit will track down only to $129 billion in 1993.

---

* Professor of Economics, Princeton University.

That is not as bad as it sounds. A lot of us here in America just haven't gotten used to big numbers yet. In 1993, $129 billion will be about 1.8 percent of projected GNP. That is not out of line with historical norms—which is another way of saying that $129 billion in 1993 won't be what it was in 1982, but rather a quite different, and much smaller, animal.

As against those two numbers for the fiscal 1993 deficit—zero as the Gramm-Rudman target and $129 billion as the CBO projection—attention is often focussed on the estimated $103 billion OASDI surplus in that same fiscal year. That sounds like another big number.

Two things must be said about that. First, the $103 billion includes the trust fund's interest earnings, which are simply paid from one government account to another government account and have nothing at all to do with the overall fiscal deficit and therefore nothing at all to do with the balance of saving and investment in the economy. To see that this is true, just imagine that the Treasury ceased paying interest to the Social Security trust fund. The unified budget deficit would not change. If you deduct the interest, the contribution of Social Security to reducing the fiscal year 1993 deficit is on the order of $65 billion, roughly two-thirds of the number we started with.

The second reason that the Social Security surplus is not such a big deal is that we are not starting from zero in 1989 but from a rather big number—again, on a net-of-interest basis—about $45 billion. So the difference between now and four years from now in terms of what Social Security contributes to helping alleviate the deficit problem is about $20 billion—not much over four years.

On the other hand, it is not nothing; and every little bit helps. I am of the opinion, for many of the reasons that Carol Cox and Jim Jones elucidated, that a little bit more help from Social Security is probably in order. And I am also of the opinion that, for many of the reasons that were mentioned, taxing benefits is the right first step.

The point I want to make is that, from a macroeconomic perspective, the current Gramm-Rudman-Hollings target for fiscal 1993, which amounts to a deficit in the non-Social Security part of the budget of about one percent of GNP, seems about right to me. No one knows if the right target is one percent, one-half of a percent, or one and one half percent of GNP. But one percent seems in the right ballpark.

The problem, of course, is getting there. My own feeling, not as an economist but as an amateur political psychoanalyst, is that making the 1993 target just a tad more attainable is probably a good thing in the current political environment. This is much the same attitude I have when I tell my sons to clean up their rooms. I never insist that the rooms be spotless, for then they'd give up the effort. I have an agreement, for example, with my older son that a maximum of one wet towel can be on his floor at any one time. It works fairly well; usually there is one. When I tried to go to zero wet towels, it didn't work; I had much more success with one. So I think we should thank Social Security for making Congress's job easier.

Now, what about the long run, which is really a much more interesting problem? A great deal has been written about how the annual Social Security surpluses—which always include interest—will lead to a huge trust fund accumulation between now and the year 2020 or 2030, building up to, perhaps, 30 percent of GNP. On some reasonable forecast—is it an oxymoron to think of a "reasonable macroeconomic forecast" fifty years ahead?—that might be in the neighborhood of the entire national debt. That sounds like a huge event, a revolution in the fiscal posture, as do projections of annual Social Security surpluses in excess of $500 billion sometime in the early part of the next century.

But I want to make the same two points I made before. First, much of that is interest, and indeed, by the time we get to around the year 2018 or so, *all* of it is interest. By then, there will be no non-interest surplus coming from Social Security anymore. Second, the GNP is also going to be a titanic number by then. So, a $12 trillion trust fund, which sounds like a colossal number, will simply not be that large. In fact, the largest annual excess of taxes over benefits (excluding interest) is projected to be about one and one-quarter percent of GNP. That happens sometime early in the next century. A one and one-quarter percent of GNP shift in the fiscal posture is very far from a revolutionary change.

But, as I said before, neither is it trivial; and it would, in my judgment, be very, very welcome. If we could get the non-Social Security deficit down to around one and one-quarter percent of GNP, which is fairly close to its historic norm, and then put on top of that about a one and one-quarter percent surplus from the Social Security piece, then we would have the overall budget in approximate balance—which means that the debt-to-GNP ratio would be falling at the rate of nominal GNP growth, perhaps 7 percent per year. That would be a great improvement, I think, over where we are now. We would have a tighter budget and looser monetary policy while maintaining nominal GNP growth at current rates. I, like most economists, judge that to be a vastly superior policy mix. It would lead to lower interest rates, and probably (there is a little uncertainty here because of foreign capital flows) to a somewhat higher investment/GNP ratio, and certainly to balance or perhaps to a surplus in our international trade. I think all this would be most welcome, not only in the United States but also in the rest of the world.

So, in my judgment, a shift from where we are now to overall budget balance would be a very, very good thing—especially since America is such a chronically low-saving society. And Social Security will help make that shift happen—so long as we don't spend the Social Security surpluses.

Once again speaking as an amateur political psychoanalyst, not as an economist, saving the funds strikes me as much, much easier to do if Social Security is really taken out of the budget after fiscal year 1993. Until then, Social Security is functionally very much on-budget. I would like to see OASDI truly off the budget at the end of the Gramm-Rudman horizon.

Like all good economists, however, I am two-handed. One possible exception to the don't-spend-the-surpluses rule that I have just enunciated can, I think, be given a coherent intellectual defense. It was first defended to me, quite well in fact, by Isabel Sawhill, and Hugh Heclo just supported the same view. The view is that it might make sense to take the coming surpluses in the Social Security trust fund and spend them on things like public infrastructure or human capital investment. What do I mean by "things like"? I mean things that will raise future labor productivity, thereby raising future wages, thereby raising the future tax base of the Social Security system. If we did that, we would not be simply eating the acorns that we need to squirrel away for the years after 2020, but in fact would be taking positive actions to make sure that American real wages are higher after the year 2020.

As I say, I think that is an intellectually defensible position. However, these human capital and public infrastructure investments must be *new marginal* investments. They cannot just be the same things we would be doing anyway, papered over by a financing arrangement that makes them look as if they are now being paid for by Social Security. We don't just want a lot of paper transactions that give the appearance—but not the substance—of doing more investment. That would be neither intellectually nor politically defensible. If we just take the Social Security money and use it to pay the bills for investments we would be making anyway, then we will just be consuming the Social Security nest egg.

However, when I return to my role as a political psychoanalyst, rather than as an economist, it seems to me that the latter is exactly what we would do. That is, we would do the paper transactions needed to assign Social Security funds to infrastructure but would not actually spend more on schools, roads, or bridges. We would just pretend we had used the Social Security money for these wonderful purposes. As I see it, speaking once again as a political psychoanalyst, it is better not to create that temptation for Congress in the first place.

CLOSING REMARKS
The Honorable Daniel Patrick Moynihan*

I AM VERY PLEASED TO BE HERE ON THE OCCASION OF the First Annual Conference of the National Academy of Social Insurance.

I begin with a note of thanks to the National Academy for its recently released study on the Social Security "notch" issue. Senator Dole and I requested the study to help educate Finance Committee members on this extremely complex and often misunderstood subject, and we are much indebted for the excellent and lucid work of Bob Myers and others.

The National Academy of Social Insurance has come just when needed. The remarkable group who built Social Security is now collecting it. An institutional memory is vitally needed to guide us through the issues confronting our most important domestic program.

The development of the Social Security Act was a very close matter, as we know from the careful work of Edwin Witte, Martha Derthick, and others. It was the product of the very dedicated work of a small group of public-spirited men and women under the leadership of Frances Perkins. It is hard to overstate the contribution of that woman, who not only set up the Committee on Economic Security and brought in people who figured out a program, but also got the program past the Supreme Court. This was no small feat, given that the Court had struck down as unconstitutional most of the Roosevelt administration's more modest first-term New Deal initiatives. In her book *The Roosevelt I Knew,* Ms. Perkins says, "I drew courage from a bit of advice I got accidentally from Supreme Court Justice Stone." She didn't get it accidentally at all. At a reception she asked this man something you're not supposed to ask a Supreme Court Justice, which was how he would rule if we enacted a national social insurance program by

* United States Senator from New York and Chairman of the Subcommittee on Social Security and Family Policy, Senate Finance Committee.

using this approach or that approach, the Congress's commerce power or taxing power. In response to which, she writes, Justice Stone whispered, "The taxing power of the Federal Government, my dear; the taxing power is sufficient for everything you want and need." And that is why Social Security is a subcommittee of the tax-writing committees of the House and Senate.

But the time has come to open up what has been a very closely held public trust and to improve the public discussion and understanding of Social Security, and of course this is another very important purpose of the National Academy of Social Insurance. Earlier this week, the *Washington Post* referred to the Social Security program as "one of the greatest governmental success stories of this century," which, as we all know, is true. And yet people don't believe it. They have no confidence in the system. Attempts by the Reagan administration to cut benefits naturally have contributed to this lack of confidence. As early as 1981 the then newly appointed Director of the Office of Management and Budget was declaring, with respect to the trust funds, that the "most devastating bankruptcy in history" was months away. This, of course, was never true—at worst, checks would have gone out a couple of days late—but it served to justify the Administration's 1981 proposals for massive Social Security cuts. And then in 1985 we saw Vice President George Bush cast the tie-breaking vote in the Senate to cut the COLA.

But the truth is, this lack of confidence actually was evident before all that. In 1979, Peter D. Hart Research Associates conducted a nationwide survey for the National Commission on Social Security. The survey was designed to determine the public's attitude toward Social Security and it found that 61 percent of the non-retired had little confidence that funds would be available to pay their retirement benefits. Sadly, the public's confidence had sunk even lower by 1985, when a survey by Yankelovich, Skelly & White showed that 66 percent, two-thirds, of non-retired adults thought it unlikely that they would ever see their benefits—two-thirds! Now I understand that the American Council of Life Insurance has just this month published some data that indicate an improvement in 1988. I haven't seen these data. I welcome the news, but I put it to you that the lack of public confidence remains the biggest problem facing Social Security. The system is, after all, a compact across generations. The willingness of young workers to fund the program rests on the confidence that it will be there for them when they need it.

We had this in mind in twelve days in January 1983, when we developed the plan that put Social Security on a sound financial footing for the next seventy-five years. I served on the National Commission on Social Security Reform, along with Bob Ball, the former and revered Social Security

Commissioner and Chairman of the Academy, Bob Dole, Barber Conable, Alan Greenspan, and others. We wanted to build a reserve in the trust funds that people could see and believe in, and we are building such a reserve. Today the trust funds are growing at the rate of $110 million a day and rising. The reserve will top $100 billion this month and grow to $11.8 trillion by 2030. In those twelve days in January we may have built better than we knew.

Of course, efforts to cut Social Security in the spirit of budget-cutting still undermine confidence in the system, and are still very much a part of the political landscape. Recently Presidents Carter and Ford suggested in their "American Agenda" that we should cut the COLA formula to the CPI minus two, to help reduce the deficit. I am perplexed and disappointed every time I see this proposal and am often surprised at some of the names I see associated with it. Over a ten-year period, this would result in an 18 percent benefit cut. This simply cannot be justified in the name of deficit reduction. Social Security is a self-financed system in surplus. If we cut benefits we must cut the dedicated payroll taxes, and that doesn't help reduce the deficit. So cutting Social Security is simply not the answer to our budget problem, and discussing such cuts just leaves the American public uncertain about the future of this great and successful program.

Oddly, the surpluses we established to build confidence in the system have of late been the subject of some derision in the popular literature of the business community. An article in the August 1988 issue of Fortune begins:

> Enter the strange world of Social Security, as exotically inside out as the domain of black holes and anti-matter that physicists describe.

The article goes on to describe how trust fund assets are really just "IOUs" from the Treasury. What is interesting here is how those IOUs, when they sit in the vaults of Morgan Stanley, become the most solid and respected long-term investments you can have in your portfolio. But this is the kind of lingering skepticism we are up against.

This is why I am happy to see the Academy addressing the issue of the trust fund surpluses with its First Annual Conference. This matter of the trust funds and their proper relationship to the budget will be one of the most important Social Security and budget issues for the next several years. It is of the utmost importance that the next Congress and Administration understand this issue and understand it well, because we have some important decisions to make. We face the opportunity to quadruple our saving rate and get back on a path of economic growth, if we can tackle the general fund deficit problem and stop spending our Social Security surpluses on current government consumption.

The problem is simple, really—we don't save enough. In the 1950s, '60s, and '70s our net national saving as a percent of net national product ran about 8 percent. In 1987 it was 2 percent. The components of national saving are, of course, private saving and government saving. Net private saving of 6.1 percent of net national product were offset by a Federal budget deficit of 4.1 percent in 1987. Put another way, the deficit ate up the equivalent of two-thirds of our private saving that year. How did we finance our domestic investment? Mostly on money borrowed from abroad.

To increase investment and economic growth, we must balance or bring much closer to balance the non-Social Security budget and dedicate our Social Security surpluses to increased saving. This, of course, Gramm-Rudman-Hollings does not envision—it seeks only to balance, in 1993, the budget inclusive of the trust funds. We must go farther than this. In the current fiscal year, a $52 billion Social Security surplus will help to mask a $199 billion deficit in the operating budget, according to Congressional Budget Office estimates. I plan to introduce legislation in the 101st Congress to establish new deficit reduction targets that do not include the Social Security trust funds so we can get about the business of balancing the non-Social Security budget.

I am not naive about the politics of this. But this is an extremely important matter, this opportunity we have to secure a better economic future, and we must try hard not to blow it. If we try and fail, then we have to give some serious consideration to lowering Social Security taxes and not running these trust fund surpluses, as our friend Bob Myers has suggested, because it would not be advisable to run these Social Security surpluses only to spend the money on other government programs. But let us not give up before we have started. The opportunity is at hand, and we know what we must do. We must begin by getting the word out. I have requested a report from the General Accounting Office on the budgetary and economic issues associated with the Social Security surpluses, and this is scheduled for release next month, just in time for the new Congress and Administration. And I am hopeful that the National Academy of Social Insurance will continue its excellent effort, represented by this conference, to educate policymakers and the public on these important issues. This kind of informed discussion is essential if we hope to do the right thing, and, as ever, doing the right thing is essential if we hope to restore confidence in the Social Security program.

There are other things we can do to improve public confidence in Social Security, and we must devote ourselves to these wholeheartedly. I have a couple of ideas, and I am always open to more. I plan to reintroduce my bill to require the Social Security Administration to send annual statements to all workers covered by Social Security, telling them what they have paid in and what they can expect to get back in the way of benefits. I believe that one of the reasons the public lacks confidence in Social Security is that we never hear from the Social Security Administration until we become beneficiaries, even though we see money withheld for Social Security from every paycheck. The Canadian government started sending out Social Security earnings and benefit statements a few years ago, and they say the program has been extremely successful in improving public understanding of their system. I am sure we could expect the same result here.

I will also be reintroducing my bill to make the Social Security Administration an independent agency. As many of you know, this bill would remove SSA from the Department of Health and Human Services and have the independent agency administered by a bipartisan board, as it was originally. There is much popular and political support for this idea, evidenced by the fact that a similar bill passed the House unanimously in 1986. This restructuring would improve the public's confidence in the program by insulating it from the kind of partisan politics it has been subjected to in recent years, and I think we can get this taken care of in the coming Congress.

There is one other item on my Social Security legislative agenda, and that is to get a Federal charter for the National Academy of Social Insurance. I got this through the Senate this year as part of the Tax Technicals bill, but the conference ran into a jurisdictional problem on the House side. I am confident we can work this out, though. I will be reintroducing this bill in the Senate, and Andy Jacobs, chairman of the House Social Security subcommittee, has assured me that he will sponsor it in the House. This charter will assist the National Academy in its important work of promoting the study and understanding of Social Security.

ABOUT THE PRESENTERS

Henry J. Aaron is a Senior Fellow at The Brookings Institution and a Professor of Economics at the University of Maryland. He is also a member of the Board of Directors of Abt Associates, Inc., and a Senior Associate of the Policy Economics Group of Peat, Marwick, and Main, Inc. Formerly, Mr. Aaron served as Assistant Secretary for Planning and Evaluation at the Department of Health, Education, and Welfare and Chair of the 1979 Advisory Council on Social Security. Mr. Aaron is the author or coauthor of 10 books and over 50 publications or chapters in books. His most recent publication is *Can America Afford to Grow Old? Paying For Social Security.* Mr. Aaron received his Ph.D. in economics at Harvard University.

Robert M. Ball served as Commissioner of Social Security from 1962 to 1973, under Presidents Kennedy, Johnson and Nixon. He was also a member of President Reagan's National Commission on Social Security Reform. Mr. Ball began working for the Social Security Administration in 1939 and has been an active participant in policymaking ever since. From 1973 to 1981, Mr. Ball was a Senior Scholar at the Institute of Medicine and from 1981 to 1988 a Visiting Scholar at the Center for the Study of Social Policy. Currently, Mr. Ball is the Chair of the National Academy of Social Insurance. Mr. Ball, author of *Social Security: Today and Tomorrow,* has written extensively on Social Security and frequently testifies before Congress. Mr. Ball received his undergraduate degree and a M.A. in economics from Wesleyan College.

Alan S. Blinder is the Gordon S. Rentschler Memorial Professor of Economics and Chair of the Economics Department at Princeton University. He is also the Vice President of the American Economic Association. Professor Blinder is a columnist for *Business Week* and the author of several books including the recently published *Hard Heads, Soft Hearts: Tough-Minded Economics for a Just Society.* Professor Blinder testifies frequently on economic policy before Congress, was formerly the Deputy Assistant Director, Fiscal Analysis Division at the Congressional Budget Office (1975), and continues to work as a consultant with the Congressional Budget Office. Professor Blinder received his Ph.D. from the Massachusetts Institute of Technology.

Fay Lomax Cook is an Associate Professor of Social Policy at Northwestern University. In addition, she serves on the Publications Committee and the Executive Committee of the Gerontological Society of America and on the Research Advisory Committee of the Chicago Urban League. In 1987–88 Professor Cook was a Visiting Scholar at the Russell Sage Foundation. She is the author of *Who Should be Helped? Public Support for Social Services* and numerous articles and papers on social policy, elderly issues and public opinion. Professor Cook received her M.A. and Ph.D. in social welfare policy at the University of Chicago.

Carol G. Cox is President of Carol Cox and Associates, a Washington consulting firm which advises and represents corporations, businesses and individuals on public policy issues, with an emphasis on economics, the budget and tax policy. Mrs. Cox is also President and Executive Officer of the Committee for a Responsible Federal Budget, a nonprofit, bipartisan organization formed to educate the public on the federal budget and the budget process. In addition, Mrs. Cox served as a consultant to the National Economic Commission. She has written numerous articles on the budget and has published "Op-Ed" pieces in the *Washington Post* and the *Los Angeles Times*. Mrs. Cox is a graduate of Whittier College.

Hugh Heclo is the Clarence J. Robinson Professor at George Mason University and former Professor of Government at Harvard University. He teaches courses in American national politics and social welfare policy. Currently, Professor Heclo serves as Chair of the Ford Foundation's Research Committee on "Social Welfare and the American Future." Professor Heclo is the author of several award-winning books including *Modern Social Politics* which received the Woodrow Wilson award from the American Political Science Association as the best book published in the United States in 1974 on government, politics or international affairs. Professor Heclo received his Ph.D. in political science from Yale University.

John Heinz is the senior United States Senator from Pennsylvania. He was first elected to the Senate in 1976. Previously he served in the U.S. House of Representatives (1971–76). Senator Heinz is Ranking Minority Member of the Senate Special Committee on Aging. He was named one of the ten most effective legislators on behalf of the elderly by *50 Plus* magazine. The Senator was a member of the 1983 National Commission on Social Security Reform. In addition, he was Chair of the National Republican Senatorial Committee for the 1979–80 election and again for the 1985–86 election. Senator Heinz received his B.A. from Yale University and his M.B.A. from Harvard University.

James Jones is currently a partner in the Washington law firm of Dickstein, Shapiro and Morin. In addition, he serves on the Board of Governors for the American Stock Exchange and the Board of Directors of The Equitable Life Assurance Society of the United States. Mr. Jones was a United States Representative from Oklahoma for fourteen years. During his tenure in office, he served as Chairman of the House Budget Committee and of the Social Security Subcommittee. Prior to that, Mr. Jones was White House Chief of Staff for President Lyndon B. Johnson. Mr. Jones received his law degree from Georgetown University and his undergraduate degree from the University of Oklahoma.

Karlyn Keene is the Managing Editor of *Public Opinion* magazine, the flagship publication of the American Enterprise Institute. She joined the Institute in 1979 and was made a Resident Fellow in 1983. In 1985, Ms. Keene was selected as one of six fellows at Harvard University's Institute of Politics. Prior to that, Ms. Keene worked for a public relations firm and a United States Senator. Ms. Keene has written on many different public opinion topics including the gender gap, the political impact of the baby boom generation, the "fairness" issue in American politics and the Federal government's role in our society. Ms. Keene is a graduate of the University of Wisconsin.

Robert Kuttner is economics correspondent of the *New Republic* and a contributing columnist to *Business Week* and the *The Boston Globe*. In addition, his work frequently appears in the *The New York Times, The Los Angeles Times* and the *Washington Post*. Mr. Kuttner's most recent book, *The Life of the Party*, was published in 1987. At Harvard University, Mr. Kuttner has been a Kennedy Fellow at the John F. Kennedy School of Government and taught seminars at Harvard's Institute of Politics. He taught journalism at Boston University and for the 1987-88 academic year was a visiting professor at the University of Massachusetts. Mr. Kuttner received his undergraduate degree from Oberlin College and his M.A. in political science from Berkeley.

Phillip J. Longman is currently a staff writer for *Florida Trend* magazine and has been published in *Atlantic, Esquire,* the *New Republic, The New York Times Magazine, the Wall Street Journal* and the *Washington Monthly*. In 1987 and 1988 Mr. Longman was chief speech writer and policy analyst for Congressman Kenneth MacKay. Prior to his work on Capitol Hill, Mr. Longman was research director for Americans for Generational Equity. Mr. Longman is also the author of *Born to Pay: The New Politics of Aging in America*. Mr. Longman received his B.A. in philosophy from Oberlin College.

Daniel Patrick Moynihan is the senior United States Senator from New York. He was first elected to the Senate in 1976. He is Chairman of the Subcommittee on Social Security and Family Policy of the Senate Finance Committee. The Senator was a member of the 1983 National Commission on Social Security Reform. Senator Moynihan was a member of the

Cabinet or Sub-Cabinet of Presidents Kennedy, Johnson, Nixon and Ford. He is the author or editor of 14 books, including, most recently, *Came the Revolution: Argument in the Reagan Era*. The Senator is a regent of the Smithsonian Institution and the recipient of 55 honorary degrees. Senator Moynihan received his B.A. from Tufts University and his Ph.D. from the Fletcher School of Law and Diplomacy.

Norman Ornstein is a Resident Scholar at the American Enterprise Institute for Public Policy Research. He is also a political contributor to the MacNeil/Lehrer Newshour and an election analyst for CBS news. Formerly, Mr. Ornstein held various positions on Capitol Hill and was a professor of politics at Catholic University. In addition, Mr. Ornstein was the series editor and co-host of *Congress: We the People*, an award-winning 26-part television series. Mr. Ornstein's recent publications include *The American Elections of 1982* and *The New Congress*. Mr. Ornstein received his M.A. and Ph.D. from the University of Michigan.

Rudolph G. Penner is a Senior Fellow at The Urban Institute and former director of the Congressional Budget Office. Prior to that, he was Assistant Director for Economic Policy at the Office of Management and Budget, Deputy Assistant Secretary for Economic Affairs at the Department of Housing and Urban Development, and Senior Staff Economist for the Council of Economic Advisers. Mr. Penner is the author of *Social Security Financing Proposals* and *The Budget in Transition*. Mr. Penner received his Ph.D. in economics from The Johns Hopkins University.

Charles L. Schultze is the Director of the Economic Studies Program at The Brookings Institution. He has been a visiting professor at the National University in Singapore and Stanford University and has taught at the University of Maryland and Indiana University. Mr. Schultze was Chairman of the Council of Economic Advisers from 1977–1980 and Director of the U.S. Bureau of the Budget, 1962–1964. In addition, Mr. Schultze was president of the American Economic Association in 1984. He received his B.A. and M.A. from Georgetown University and his Ph.D. from the University of Maryland.

John B. Shoven has been a faculty member in the Economics Department at Stanford University since 1973 and is currently Chair of the Department. In addition, he is Director of the Center for Economic Policy Research and Co-Director of the National Bureau of Economic Research. Professor Shoven has done long-term work with the Office of Tax Analysis of the U.S. Treasury Department and consulting with the Department of Labor, the President's Council of Economic Advisers, the Federal Reserve Board and the World Bank. Professor Shoven received his Ph.D. in economics from Yale University.

Lawrence H. Thompson currently serves as Assistant Comptroller General in charge of the Human Resources Division of the U.S. General Accounting Office and was formerly Chief Economist at GAO. Prior to that, Mr. Thompson worked for nine years on income security issues for the Department of Health and Human Services. This included service as Director of Social Security Planning in the Office of the Secretary of HHS, Executive Director of the 1979 Advisory Council on Social Security, and Associate Social Security Commissioner for Policy. Mr. Thompson received a M.B.A. from the Wharton School of the University of Pennsylvania and a Ph.D. from the University of Michigan.